P9-BXV-884

CHURCH LAW & TAX REPORT

The 2004 Compensation Handbook for Church Staff

James F. Cobble, Jr., D.Min., Ed.D. & Richard R. Hammar, J.D., LL.M., CPA

Christian Ministry Resources

PO Box 1098

Matthews, NC 28106

(704) 821-3845

Fax (704) 821-3872

www.churchlawtoday.com

This publication is designed to provide accurate and authoritative information in regard to the subject matter covered. It is sold with the understanding that the publisher is not engaged in rendering legal, accounting, or other professional service. If legal advice or other expert assistance is required, the services of a competent professional person should be sought. "From a Declaration of Principles jointly adopted by a Committee of the American Bar Association and a Committee of Publishers and Associations."

Table of Contents

1. Introduction 5

2. Compensation Planning 7

3. Using the Compensation Tables 24

4. Compensation Profiles: General Comparisons . . . 30

5 Senior Pastors 39

6. Associate Pastors 53

7. Christian Education Directors 67

8. Youth Ministers 78

9. Choir and Music Directors 89

10. Church Administrators 100

11. Church Bookkeepers 111

12. Church Secretaries 122

13. Church Custodians 133

14. Statistical Abstract of Participating Churches . . 144

Appendix 1: Eight Year Compensation Trend . . . 148

Appendix 2: Compensation and Church Income . . . 149

Appendix 3: Compensation and Church Attendance . . 150

Appendix 4: Compensation Averages by Education . . 151

Appendix 5: Standard Deviation Ranges for
Pastoral Compensation Based on Church Income . . 152

Chapter 1

Introduction

Welcome to *The 2004 Compensation Handbook for Church Staff*. Please take a few minutes to read this introduction. It provides several ways to maximize your use of this book.

The *Compensation Handbook* was developed to provide church leaders and employees with a current and reliable picture of compensation practices across a broad spectrum of American churches. It presents survey data from nearly 2,700 churches representing approximately 8,500 staff members. The survey data was obtained between January, 2003 and April, 2003 from churches that subscribe to *Church Law & Tax Report*, *Church Treasurer Alert!*, or *Church Secretary Today*. This information can play an important role in determining equitable compensation packages for church staff members. The *Compensation Handbook* can help you:

- ⮂ to determine appropriate compensation levels for nine key pastoral, professional, and support staff positions.

- ⮂ to develop effective compensation packages—guidelines are given to maximize net income while remaining in compliance with federal tax laws.

- ⮂ to provide church workers with a statistical framework for evaluating their present compensation package—comparisons can be made regarding church size, budget, setting, and other important variables.

- ⮂ to develop an objective standard for evaluating requests for raises and changes in benefits.

- ⮂ to assist denominational offices and other ecclesiastical organizations in promoting equitable and fair compensation practices within their churches.

- ⮂ to better understand the nature of church compensation planning.

How To Make The Best Use Of This Book

Anyone engaged in compensation planning for church staff members should first become familiar with some basic federal tax laws. How a compensation package is structured can either help or hurt a church staff member. Chapter 2 provides a detailed discussion of the major tax laws that affect the compensation of church staff, and provides tax saving tips.

Chapter 3 provides guidance on reading and using the data found in the tables throughout this book. Included is an example that illustrates how to determine compensation ranges for a senior pastor. The same process can be used for all staff positions.

5

Chapter 4 provides comparisons between the national averages of the nine staff positions included in this study. The chapter begins by providing an employment profile for each staff position. Table 4-3 provides a comparative ranking of each position along with the standard deviation for each national average. Standard deviation is an important statistical calculation that is explained in both chapters 3 and 4. Denominational comparisons are also presented in this chapter.

Chapters 5-13 provide detailed information on each individual staff position. Natural curiosity will pull most church staff members immediately to the chapter which presents data about their position. Remember, though, understanding chapters 2 and 3 is critical to using this book in an effective manner.

Finally, chapter 14 provides a statistical abstract of the churches participating in this study. A graphical representation of the data is found in the appendices.

Data Analysis

Inconclusive or faulty survey data were not included in the survey. Figures that appeared unrealistic or way outside the normal distribution were eliminated to avoid skewing the results. These results represent the churches that participated in the survey. The sampling population used was a fair representation of American churches, but certain church sizes, budget sizes, and denominations have a stronger representation than others. To the extent possible, we have attempted to organize the data in ways that avoid small samples. At times, however, small samples simply reflect a reality such as rural churches with an attendance over 1,000, or churches smaller than 100 with a full-time business administrator. Nevertheless, sample size should be taken into account when considering the value of any particular finding. Standard deviations were calculated for the average compensation of each position. Some variables, however, reflected more of a linear relationship with compensation than did others. That relationship also changed from one position to another. The Pearson product-moment correlation coefficient was calculated to determine the strength of relationship between compensation and church size, and compensation and church budget for each of the nine positions. Coefficients of determination and nondetermination were also calculated to gain a better intuitive notion of the strength of the relationships between size and compensation, and budget and compensation. While this study does not make explicit reference to those findings, they do provide the basis for the inferences made at various points within the text about correlations.

Chapter 2

Compensation Planning

Synopsis. Compensation planning for clergy and other church staff presents several unique issues that are not well understood by many church leaders and their advisers. This chapter clears away the confusion and presents 19 key considerations to review while doing compensation planning.

Most churches will adopt year 2004 compensation packages for their ministers and lay staff members in the final months of 2003. Now is a good time to review several possible components of a compensation package. Consider the following.

1. Salary. The most basic component of church staff compensation is salary. There are two important considerations to keep in mind with respect to staff salaries—the amount of the salary, and the use of "salary reduction agreements." These two issues will be discussed separately.

a. Amount. Staff salaries ordinarily are set by the church board. Churches generally may pay any amount they wish, with one very big exception—if a church pays unreasonably high compensation to a pastor or other employee there are two possible consequences:

(1) Loss of tax-exempt status. In order for a church or any other charity to maintain its tax-exempt status it must meet a number of conditions. One condition is that it cannot pay unreasonably high compensation to any person. There are two considerations to note. First, very few charities have lost their exempt status for paying unreasonable compensation. The IRS has been very reluctant to impose this remedy. Few if any legitimate churches have lost their exempt status on this ground. Second, the law does not define what amount of compensation is unreasonable, and neither the IRS nor the courts have provided much clarification.

> ☞ **Example.** One federal appeals court concluded that combined annual income of $115,680 paid by a religious organization to its founder and his wife was *not* excessive.

> ☞ **Example.** The court in the "PTL" bankruptcy case concluded that maximum reasonable compensation for Jim Bakker would have been $133,100 in 1984, $146,410 in 1985, $161,051 in 1986, and $177,156 in 1987. The court based its conclusions on a comparison of the salaries of other nonprofit officers in the state.

(2) Intermediate sanctions. The IRS can assess "intermediate sanctions" against employees of churches and other charities who are paid "excess benefits" (defined as unreasonable compensation). Note that the IRS still can revoke the exempt status of any charity that pays excessive compensation to an employee. However, it is now more likely that excessive compensation will result in intermediate sanctions rather than loss of exempt status. To illustrate, why should a major university lose its tax-exempt status because it pays excessive compensation to its football coach?

It is very important for church leaders to be familiar with intermediate sanctions, since the law allows the IRS to assess large penalties against both highly compensated persons and members of a governing board who authorized the excessive compensation. The intermediate sanctions the IRS can impose include the following:

● *Tax on disqualified persons.* A "disqualified person" (someone, like a senior pastor, with significant administrative responsibilities) who benefits from an excess benefit transaction is subject to an excise tax equal to 25 percent of the amount of the "excess benefit" (the amount by which actual compensation exceeds the fair market value of services rendered). This tax is assessed against the disqualified person directly, not his or her employer.

● *Additional tax on disqualified persons.* If a disqualified person fails to "correct" the excess benefit by the time the IRS assesses the 25 percent tax, then the IRS can assess an additional tax of 200 percent of the excess benefit. The law specifies that a disqualified person can "correct" the excess benefit transaction by "undoing the excess benefit to the extent possible, and taking any additional measures necessary to place the organization in a financial position not worse than that in which it would be if the disqualified person were dealing under the highest fiduciary standards."

● *Tax on organization managers.* If the IRS assesses the 25 percent tax against a disqualified person, it is permitted to impose an additional 10 percent tax (up to a maximum of $10,000) on any "organization manager" who participates in an excess benefit transaction knowing it is such a transaction, unless the manager's participation "is not willful and is due to reasonable cause." A "manager" is an officer, director, or trustee. IRS regulations clarify that the managers collectively cannot be liable for more than $10,000 for any one transaction.

> ⟡ **Key point.** The intermediate sanctions law imposes an excise tax on members of a church's governing board who vote for a compensation package that the IRS determines to be excessive. This makes it essential for board members to carefully review the reasonableness of compensation packages.

Charities, disqualified persons, and governing boards may rely on a "presumption of reasonableness" with respect to a compensation arrangement if it was approved by a board of directors (or committee of the board) that: (1) was composed entirely of individuals unrelated to and not subject to the control of the disqualified person involved in the arrangement; (2) obtained and relied upon objective "comparability" information, such as (a) compensation paid by similar organizations, both taxable and tax-exempt, for comparable positions, (b) independent compensation surveys by nationally recognized independent firms, or (c) actual written offers from similar institutions competing for the services of the disqualified person; and (3) adequately documented the basis for its decision.

> ⟡ **Key point.** The law creates a presumption that a minister's compensation package is reasonable if approved by a church board that relied upon objective "comparability" information, including independent compensation surveys by nationally recognized independent firms. The most comprehensive compensation survey for church workers is this text. This means that most ministers will be able to use this text to establish the presumption of reasonableness. But it also suggests that the IRS will rely on the data in this text in any attempt to impose intermediate sanctions against ministers.

IRS regulations clarify that "revenue based pay" arrangements in which an employee's compensation is based on a percentage of the employer's total revenues do not automatically result in an excess benefit transaction triggering intermediate sanctions. Rather, "all relevant facts and circumstances" must be considered.

⊃ **Recommendation.** Churches that pay a minister (or any staff member) more than two standard deviations above the national average for comparable positions should obtain a legal opinion from an experienced tax attorney confirming that the amount paid is not "unreasonable" and will not expose the employee or the board to intermediate sanctions. See chapter 4 for a discussion of standard deviations.

✎ **Tax savings tip.** Ministers and other church staff members should carefully review their W-2 or 1099 to be sure that it does not report more income than was actually received. If an error was made, the church should issue a corrected tax form (Form W-2c for an employee, or a "corrected" Form 1099 for a self-employed worker).

b. Salary reduction agreements. Many churches have established "salary reduction agreements" to handle certain staff expenses. The objective is to reduce a worker's taxable income, since only the income remaining after the various "reductions" is reported on the worker's W-2 or 1099 form at the end of the year. It is important for churches to understand that they cannot reduce a worker's taxable income through salary reductions unless specifically allowed by law.

Here are three ways that taxable income can be reduced through salary reduction agreements:

(1) *Tax-sheltered annuity contributions.* Salary reduction agreements can be used to contribute to a tax-sheltered annuity (sometimes called a "403(b) annuity), if the salary reductions meet certain conditions.

(2) *"Cafeteria plans."* Salary reduction agreements also can be used to fund "cafeteria plans" (including "flexible spending arrangements") if several conditions are met. A cafeteria plan is a written plan established by an employer that allows employees to choose between cash and a "menu" of nontaxable benefits specified by law (including employer-provided medical insurance premiums, group-term life insurance, and dependent care).

(3) *Housing allowances.* A church can designate a portion of a minister's salary as a housing allowance, and the amount so designated is not subject to income tax if certain conditions are met. Housing allowances are addressed later in this chapter.

⊃ **Observation.** In most cases, "salary reductions" will not accomplish the goal of reducing a minister's taxable income. The income tax regulations prohibit the widespread practice of funding "accountable" reimbursement arrangements through salary reductions. This topic is addressed later in this chapter.

2. Housing allowances. The most important tax benefit available to ministers who own or rent their homes is the housing allowance. Ministers who own their home do not pay federal income taxes on the amount of their compensation that their employing church designates in advance as a housing allowance, to the extent that the allowance represents compensation for ministerial services, is used to pay housing expenses, and does not exceed the annual fair rental value of the home (furnished, plus utilities). Housing-related expenses include rent, mortgage payments, utilities, repairs, furnishings, insurance, property taxes, additions, and maintenance. Ministers who rent a home or apartment do not pay federal income taxes on the amount of their compensation that their employing church designates in advance as a housing allowance to the extent that the allowance represents compensation for ministerial services and is used to pay rental expenses such as rent, furnishings, utilities, and insurance. Unfortunately, many churches fail to designate a portion of a minister's compensation as a housing allowance. This deprives their minister of an important tax benefit.

Ministers who live in a church-owned parsonage that is provided "rent-free" as compensation for ministerial services do not include the annual fair rental value of the parsonage as income in computing their federal income taxes. The annual fair rental value is not "deducted" from the minister's income. Rather, it is not reported as additional income anywhere on Form 1040 (as it generally would be by non-clergy workers). Ministers who live in a church-provided parsonage do not pay federal income taxes on the amount of their compensation that their employing church designates in advance as a parsonage allowance, to the extent that the allowance represents compensation for ministerial services and is used to pay parsonage-related expenses such as utilities, repairs, and furnishings.

✎ **Tax savings tip.** Ministers who live in church parsonages, and who incur any out-of-pocket expenses in maintaining the parsonage (such as utilities, property taxes, insurance, furnishings, or lawn care) should be sure that their employing church designates in advance a portion of their annual compensation as a "parsonage allowance". Such an allowance is not included on the minister's W-2 or 1099 at the end of the year and is nontaxable in computing federal income taxes to the extent the minister incurs housing expenses of at least that amount. This is a very important tax benefit for ministers living in church-provided parsonages. Unfortunately, many ministers and church boards are not aware of this benefit, or are not taking advantage of it.

Note that these exclusions are for federal income tax purposes only. Ministers cannot exclude the fair rental value of a parsonage or a housing allowance when computing their self-employment (Social Security) taxes.

⊃ **Recommendation.** Ministers should be sure that the designation of a housing or parsonage allowance for year 2004 is on the agenda of the church board for one of its final meetings in 2003. The designation should be an official action of the board or congregation, and it should be duly recorded in the minutes of the meeting. The IRS also recognizes designations included in employment contracts and budget line items—assuming in each case that the designation was duly adopted by the church board (or the congregation in a business meeting).

How much should a church board or congregation designate as a housing allowance? Many churches base the allowance on their minister's estimate of actual housing expenses for the new year. The church provides the minister with a form on which anticipated housing expenses for the new year are reported. For ministers who own their homes, the form asks for projected expenses in the following categories: down payment, mortgage payments, property taxes, property insurance, utilities, furnishings and appliances, repairs and improvements, maintenance, and miscellaneous. Many churches designate an allowance in excess of the anticipated expenses itemized by the minister. Basing the allowance solely on a minister's actual expenses will penalize the minister if housing expenses in fact turn out to be higher than expected. In other words, the allowance should take into account unexpected housing costs or inaccurate projections of expenses.

⊃ **Recommendation.** Plan a mid-year review of the housing allowance to make sure that the designated amount is sufficient to cover actual expenses.

⊃ **Observation.** The compensation survey summarized over the next several chapters reveals that housing allowances are claimed by several associate ministers, administrators, music directors, secretaries, and custodians. However, it is important to note that the housing allowance is available only if two conditions are met: (1) the recipient is a minister, and (2) the allowance is provided as compensation for services performed in the exercise of ministry. In many cases, these conditions will not be satisfied by administrators, music directors, secretaries, and custodians. See chapter 3 of Richard Hammar's annual *Church and Clergy Tax Guide* (available from the publisher of this text) for more information.

3. Equity allowances. Ministers who live in church-owned parsonages are denied one very important benefit of home ownership—the opportunity to accumulate "equity" in a home over the course of many years. Many ministers who have lived in parsonages during much of their active ministry often face retirement without housing. Their fellow ministers who purchased a home early in their ministry often can look forward to retirement with a home that is either substantially or completely debt-free. To avoid the potential hardship often suffered by a minister who lives in a parsonage, some churches increase their minister's compensation by an amount sometimes referred to as an "equity allowance." The idea is to provide the minister with the equivalent of equity in a home. This is an excellent idea that should be considered by any church having one or more ministers living in church-provided housing. Of course, for the concept to work properly, the equity allowance should not be accessible by the minister until retirement. Therefore, some churches choose to place the allowance directly in a minister's tax-sheltered retirement account.

⊃ **Recommendation.** Equity allowances should also be considered by a church whose minister rents a home.

4. Accountable business expense reimbursement policy. One of the most important components of church staff compensation packages is an "accountable" business expense reimbursement arrangement. This benefit is available to both ministers and lay staff members alike. Under such an arrangement a church (1) reimburses only those business expenses that are properly substantiated within a reasonable time as to date, amount, place, and business purpose, and (2) requires any excess reimbursements (in excess of substantiated expenses) to be returned to the church. Churches should seriously consider adopting an accountable reimbursement policy for reimbursing staff business expenses. Such a policy has the following advantages:

☐ Church staff report their business expenses to the church rather than to the IRS.

☐ Church staff who report their income taxes as employees, or who report as self-employed and who are reclassified as employees by the IRS in an audit, avoid the limitations on the deductibility of employee business expenses. These limitations include (1) the elimination of any deduction if the worker cannot itemize deductions on Schedule A (most taxpayers cannot), and (2) the deductibility of business expenses on Schedule A as an itemized expense only to the extent that these expenses exceed 2% of the worker's adjusted gross income.

☐ The so-called *Deason* allocation rule is avoided. Under this rule, ministers must reduce their business expense deduction by the percentage of their total compensation that consists of a tax-exempt housing allowance.

☐ The "50% limitation" that applies to the deductibility of business meals and entertainment expenses is avoided. Unless these expenses are reimbursed by an employer under an accountable plan, only 50% of them are deductible by either employees or self-employed workers.

☐ Church staff who report their income taxes as self-employed avoid the risk of being reclassified as an employee by the IRS in an audit and assessed additional taxes.

⊃ **Observation.** The compensation survey summarized over the next several chapters reveals that many churches provide automobile allowances to their ministers and lay staff. In many cases, a church will simply provide a fixed dollar amount every month to a worker (for example, $300), and require no substantiation of business miles or a return of any "excess reimbursements" (in excess of substantiated business miles). This is referred to as a "nonaccountable" reimbursement arrangement. What are the tax consequences of such an arrangement? The allowances must be added to the worker's W-2 or 1099 at the end of the year, and the worker can claim a business deduction on Schedule A (if an employee) or on Schedule C (if self-employed). If a worker is an employee with insufficient itemized deductions to use Schedule A, there is no deduction available for business expenses even though the full amount of the monthly allowances are added to taxable income. This is a very unfortunate tax result that can be avoided completely through an accountable reimbursement arrangement. For a sample board resolution adopting an account-able business expense reimbursement arrangement, see chapter 7 of Richard Hammar's annual *Church and Clergy Tax Guide*.

The income tax regulations prohibit the funding of accountable reimbursement arrangements through salary reductions.

☞ **Example.** Assume that First Church pays Pastor Gary $500 each week, and also agrees to reimburse his substantiated business expenses for each month out of the first weekly payroll check for the following month. Assume further that Pastor Gary substantiated $300 of business expenses for January. The church issued Pastor Gary his customary check of $500 for the first week of February, but only $200 of this check represents taxable salary while the remaining $300 represents a nontaxable reimbursement under an accountable plan. Only the $200 salary component of this check is included on Pastor Gary's W-2 (or 1099) form at the end of the year. This arrangement was once common, and still is practiced by some churches. The income tax regulations do not prohibit the funding of business expense reimbursements out of salary reductions. Rather, a church's reimbursements under such arrangements cannot be "account-able." This means that a church cannot reduce W-2 income by reducing an employee's salary to pay for business expense reimbursements. In our example, the full $500 paycheck must be accumulated to Pastor Gary's W-2.

⊃ **Key point.** Many churches set aside a certain amount each year to cover an employee's total compensation. For ministers, this amount often includes salary, housing allowance, fringe benefits, and an amount for the reimbursement of business expenses. To illustrate, a church board determines in December of 2003 that Pastor Ted's compensation package for 2004 will consist of salary ($30,000), housing allowance ($10,000), fringe benefits ($5,000), and business expense reimbursements ($3,000). This is what is sometimes called a salary "restructuring" arrangement. Are such arrangements treated as salary reductions, meaning that the entire $3,000 must be accumulated to Pastor Ted's W-2 income? Not necessarily. A reasonable basis exists for not reporting the $3,000 as taxable income to Pastor Ted if all of the following conditions are met: (1) the $3,000 is used to reimburse Pastor Ted for business expenses only if the substantiation requirements of an accountable arrangement are met; (2) the salary "restructuring" occurs prior to the start of the year; (3) any undistributed portion of the $3,000 is not given to Pastor Ted at the end of the year; and (4) the church adopts two resolutions—a "compensation" resolution consisting of salary, housing, and fringe benefits, and a "business expense" resolution consisting of the $3,000 reimbursement amount. If the IRS audits Pastor Ted and asks to see the church resolution specifying his compensation, the church would produce the first resolution.

5. Travel expenses of a spouse. A church should decide if it will be paying for any of the travel expenses of a spouse accompanying a minister or other staff member on a business trip. Reimbursing these expenses represents a significant benefit. Unfortunately, there is much confusion regarding the correct reporting of such reimbursements for tax purposes. If the spouse's presence on the trip serves a legitimate business purpose, and the spouse's travel expenses are reimbursed by the church under an accountable arrangement (described above) then the reimbursements represent a nontaxable fringe benefit. If these two requirements are not met, the reimbursements represent taxable income to the minister or staff member.

▲ **Caution.** If either of these conditions is not met, then a church's reimbursement of a nonemployee spouse's travel expenses will represent taxable income to the minister or other staff member. The same applies to children who accompany a minister or staff member on a business trip.

✎ **Tax savings tip.** If a church does not reimburse the travel expenses of a pastor's spouse who accompanies the pastor on a business trip, then the spouse may be able to deduct travel expenses as a charitable contribution (assuming that the spouse's presence on the trip serves a legitimate "business" purpose).

6. Church-owned vehicles. Churches should consider the advantages of acquiring an automobile for staff members' church-related travel. Here's why. If a church purchases a car, and the church board adopts a resolution restricting use of the car to church-related activities, then the worker reports no income or deductions, and better yet, there are no accountings, reimbursements, allowances, or recordkeeping requirements. This assumes that the car is in fact used exclusively for church-related purposes, and the strict conditions specified in the income tax regulations are satisfied.

Commuting is always considered to be personal use of a car, and so this procedure would not be available if a church allowed a worker to commute to work in a church-owned vehicle. Fortunately, the income tax regulations permit certain church employees who use a church-owned vehicle exclusively for business purposes except for commuting to receive all of the benefits associated with business use of a church-owned vehicle, if certain additional conditions are met.

Unfortunately, most churches that provide a staff member with a car do not consider either of these alternatives. Rather, they simply transfer the car to the individual and impose no limitations on personal use. This arrangement results in taxable income to the staff member, whether the staff member is a minister or a lay employee. See chapter 4 of Richard Hammar's annual *Church and Clergy Tax Guide* for a full discussion of these rules.

7. Self-employment tax. Social Security benefits are financed through two tax systems. Employers and employees each pay "Social Security" and "Medicare" taxes which for 2004 amount to 7.65% of an employee's taxable wages (a total tax of 15.3%) up to a specified amount. Self-employed persons pay the "self-employment tax," which for 2004 is 15.3% of net self-employment earnings up to a specified amount. Note that self-employed workers are responsible for paying their entire Social Security tax liability, while employees pay only half (their employer pays the other half).

⊃ **Key point.** Ministers always are treated as self-employed for Social Security with respect to services performed in the exercise of their ministry, and so they do not pay "Social Security" and "Medicare" taxes. Rather, they pay the "self-employment tax" with respect to church compensation, unless they have filed a timely application for exemption from Social Security taxes (and received back a copy of their exemption application from the IRS marked "approved"). As a result, ministers must be familiar with the self-employment tax rules. So must lay church employees who work for a church that filed a timely exemption from Social Security coverage (Form 8274), since they are considered self-employed for Social Security.

Because ministers pay a much higher Social Security tax than is required of employees, many churches agree to pay a portion (i.e., one-half) of a minister's self-employment tax liability. This is perfectly appropriate. However, note that any portion of a minister's self-employment tax paid by a church must be reported as additional compensation on the minister's W-2 or 1099 form, and Form 1040. The amount paid by the church must be reported as compensation for Social Security purposes as well.

⊃ **Key point.** Housing allowances and the fair rental value of parsonages are includable in self-employment earnings for Social Security purposes.

8. Insurance. Churches often provide ministers with life, health, or disability insurance coverage and pay all of the premiums for such coverage. In some cases, churches make the same benefits available to lay staff members. The income tax regulations specify that the gross income of an *employee* does not include

> contributions which his employer makes to an accident or health plan for compensation (through insurance or otherwise) to the employee for personal injuries or sickness incurred by him, his spouse, or his dependents . . . . The employer may contribute to an accident or health plan by paying the premium (or a portion of the premium) on a policy of accident or health insurance covering one or more of his employees, or by contributing to a separate trust or fund . . . .

The exclusion of employer-paid health insurance premiums from the taxable income of employees is one of the main reasons why ministers and other staff members often are better off reporting their income taxes as employees. This important benefit is not available to workers who report their income taxes as self-employed. A church wishing to make this benefit available to its ministers (or other employees) should adopt a plan in an appropriate board resolution. Plans that benefit only ministers are exempted from the "nondiscrimination" rules that apply to most of these kinds of plans.

> ⊃ **Observation.** The compensation survey data summarized over the next several chapters reveal that many churches provide ministers with health insurance. A smaller percentage of churches provide these benefits to lay staff members. Such "discrimination" by church employers does not violate federal law.

The cost of group term life insurance bought by an employer for its employees ordinarily is not taxable to the employees so long as the amount of coverage does not exceed $50,000 per employee. Generally, life insurance can qualify as group term life insurance only if it is available to at least ten full-time employees. However, there are some exceptions to this rule. For example, the ten full-time employee rule does not apply if (1) an employer provides the insurance to all full-time employees who provide satisfactory evidence of insurability, (2) insurance coverage is based on a uniform percentage of pay, and (3) evidence of insurability is limited to a medical questionnaire completed by the employee that does not require a physical examination.

Other kinds of insurance premiums paid by the church on behalf of a minister or lay church employee ordinarily represent taxable income. For example, the cost of premiums on a whole life or universal life insurance policy paid by a church on the life of its minister (and naming the minister's spouse and children as beneficiaries) ordinarily must be reported as income to the minister.

9. Retirement accounts. Most ministers (and some lay staff members) participate in some form of retirement plan. Such plans often are sponsored either by the local church, or by a denomination or agency with which the church is affiliated. Church workers covered by certain kinds of plans can choose to have part of their pay set aside each year (through "salary reductions") in the retirement fund, rather than receiving it as income. Amounts set aside by the employing church under these plans may be excludable from gross income for tax purposes. These amounts are sometimes called "elective deferrals" because the employee elects to set aside the money, and tax on the money is deferred until it is taken out of the account. This option is available to ministers or lay workers who are covered by tax-sheltered annuities ("403(b) plans"), simplified employee pensions (SEPs), and certain other plans. Payments made by an employing church toward an employee's tax-sheltered annuity, SEP, and certain other plans, and funded out of church funds rather than through a reduction in an employee's compensation, may also be excluded from the employee's gross income for tax purposes under certain circumstances. There are limits on how much an employee can elect to contribute into such plans, and on how much the employing church can contribute out of its own funds. Of course, ministers and lay workers (whether employees or self-employed for income tax purposes) can also contribute to an IRA.

⊃ **Recommendation.** If a church has not established or contributed to a retirement plan for its staff members, then it should consider doing so or at least ensuring that staff members are participating in an adequate alternative (particularly in the case of ministers who have exempted themselves from Social Security coverage). Further, if staff members are participating in a retirement plan, then now is a good time to determine how contributions to the plan in 2004 will be funded (i.e., through employee contributions, salary reductions, or church contributions) and in what amounts.

⊃ **Key point.** Churches that have not adequately contributed to their minister's retirement, or that would like to make contributions in excess of applicable limits, should consider the possible advantages of a "rabbi trust." A church's contributions to such a trust will not be included in a minister's current taxable income, and income generated by the trust is tax-deferred. Further, a church ordinarily can contribute more toward a rabbi trust than to most other kinds of retirement program. This is very attractive for churches whose minister is approaching retirement with inadequate retirement savings. For more information see chapter 10 of Richard Hammar's annual *Church and Clergy Tax Guide*.

10. Works made for hire. It is common for church employees to compose music or write books or articles in their church office during office hours. What is often not understood is that such persons do not necessarily own the copyright in the works they create. While the one who creates a work generally is its author and the initial owner of the copyright in the work, section 201(b) of the Copyright Act specifies that "in the case of a work made for hire, the employer or other person for whom the work was prepared is considered the author . . . and, unless the parties have expressly agreed otherwise in a written instrument signed by them, owns all of the rights comprised in the copyright."

The copyright law defines "work made for hire" as "a work prepared by an employee within the scope of his or her employment." There are two requirements that must be met: (1) the person creating the work is an employee, and (2) the employee created the work within the scope of his or her employment. Whether or not one is an employee will depend on the same factors used in determining whether one is an employee or self-employed for federal income tax reporting purposes (see chapter 2 of Richard Hammar's annual *Church & Clergy Tax Guide*). However, the courts have been very liberal in finding employee status in this context, so it is possible that a court would conclude that a work is a work made for hire even though the author reports federal income taxes as a self-employed person.

The second requirement is that the work must have been created within the scope of employment. This requirement generally means that the work was created during regular working hours, on the employer's premises, using the employer's staff and equipment. This is often a difficult standard to apply. As a result, it is desirable for church employees to discuss this issue with the church leadership to avoid any potential misunderstandings. Section 201(a), quoted above, allows an employer and employee to agree in writing that copyright ownership in works created by the employee within the scope of employment belongs to the employee. This should be a matter for consideration by any church having a minister or other staff member who creates literary or musical works during office hours, on church premises, using church staff and church equipment (e.g., computers, printers, paper, library, secretaries, dictation equipment).

If a church transfers the copyright in a work made for hire to an employee, this may be viewed by the IRS as "private inurement" of the church's resources to an individual. If so, this could jeopardize the church's tax-exempt status. Neither the IRS nor any court has addressed the tax consequences of such an arrangement to a church. Here are some options:

(1) The church transfers copyright ownership to the staff member. This may constitute private inurement. When a church employee writes a book during office hours at the church, using church equipment, supplies, and personnel, the copyright in the work belongs to the church. If the church chooses to renounce its legal rights in the book, and transfers the copyright back to the employee, then it is relinquishing a potentially valuable asset that may produce royalty income for several years. Few if any churches would attempt to "value" the copyright and report it as additional taxable compensation to the employee, and as a result it is hard to avoid the conclusion that such arrangements result in inurement of the church's assets to a private individual. The legal effect is to jeopardize the church's tax-exempt status. While this risk must not be overstated, the consequences would be so undesirable that it should be taken seriously.

⊃ **Key point.** Staff members who retain ownership of a work made for hire because of a written transfer signed by the church may be subject to intermediate sanctions (discussed above). Since the church is the legal owner of the copyright in a work made for hire, it is legally entitled to any income generated from sales of the work. By letting the writer or composer retain the copyright, and all rights to royalties, the church in effect is paying compensation to that person in this amount. If the work generates substantial income, then this may trigger intermediate sanctions.

(2) The church retains the copyright. The risk of inurement can be minimized or even avoided if the church retains the copyright in works made for hire, and pays a "bonus" or some other form of compensation that is added to the author's W-2 at the end of the year. This arrangement will not jeopardize the church's tax-exempt status.

(3) The church urges employees to do "outside work" at home. Do you have a writer or composer on staff at your church? If so, it is possible that this person is doing some writing or composing on church premises, using church equipment, during office hours. One way to avoid the problems associated with work made for hire status is to encourage staff members to do all their personal writing and composing at home. Tell staff members that (1) if they do any writing or composing at church during office hours, their works may be works made for hire; (2) the church owns the copyright in such works; and (3) the church can transfer copyright to the writer or composer, but this may constitute "inurement" of the church's assets to a private individual, jeopardizing the church's tax-exempt status. By urging staff members to do all their personal writing and composing at home the church will also avoid the difficult question of whether works that are written partly at home and partly at the office are works made for hire.

(4) Sermons. Are a minister's sermons "works made for hire" that are owned by the employing church? To the extent that sermons are written in a church office, during regular church hours, using church staff and equipment, it is possible if not likely that the courts would consider them to be works made for hire.

11. Qualified Tuition Reductions ("QTRs"). Many churches operate elementary or secondary schools, and charge reduced tuition to certain school employees. For example, assume that a church operates an elementary school, charges annual tuition of $2,000, but only charges tuition of $500 for the children of school employees and charges no tuition at all for the child of Pastor Eric (the church's senior minister and president of the school). Such "tuition reductions" are perfectly appropriate. Further, section 117(d) of the federal tax code specifies that they will not result in taxable income to the school employees. In other words, a $500 annual tuition reduction awarded to a school employee whose child attends the school need not be reported as income (on the employee's W-2 or Form 1040). This obviously can be a significant benefit to school employees. However, section 117(d) also provides that "highly compensated employees" cannot exclude qualified tuition reductions from their income unless the same benefit is available on substantially similar terms to other employees. The term "highly compensated employee" is defined to include any employee who was paid compensation for the previous year in excess of a specified amount. For 2003, the amount was $90,000. The amount for 2004 was not available at the time of publication of this text.

If in the example cited above Pastor Eric was paid more than $90,000 for the previous year, then the church would have to include $2,000 (the entire amount of the tuition reduction) in Pastor Eric's reportable income since he is a highly compensated employee and the benefit available to him is not available on substantially similar terms to other employees. However, this will not affect other school employees who are not "highly compensated." They will be able to exclude tuition reductions from their income.

> ⊃ **Key point.** In 2001 the IRS ruled that tuition reductions are tax-free only for school employees, and therefore if a church operates a private school only employees who perform duties on behalf of the school qualify for this benefit. If the school offers tuition reductions to church employees who perform no duties for the school, these reductions are a taxable fringe benefit.

12. Loans to ministers. Churches often make loans to ministers to enable a minister to pay for housing or some other major purchase. In some cases the church charges no interest or a low rate far below the prevailing market rate of interest. These loans can create problems for a number of reasons. Consider the following.

> ☐ Many state nonprofit corporation laws prohibit loans to officers and directors. No church should consider making any loan (even at a reasonable rate of interest) to a minister who is an officer or director of the church without first confirming that such loans are permissible under state law.

> ☐ No-interest or low-interest loans to ministers may be viewed as "inurement" of the church's income to a minister. As noted above, this can potentially jeopardize the church's tax-exempt status.

> ☐ For loans of $10,000 or more (or for loans of lower amounts where an intent to avoid taxes exists), a church must value the benefit to a minister of receiving a no-interest or low-interest loan and add this amount to the minister's reportable income. This is a complex calculation that is beyond the scope of this book. The point is this—even if loans to ministers are allowed under your state's nonprofit corporation law, the church must recognize that no-interest and low-interest loans of $10,000 or more will result in income to a minister that must be valued and reported (on the minister's W-2 or 1099-MISC, and Form 1040). Failure to do so could result in prohibited "inurement" of the church's income to a private individual, jeopardizing the church's tax-exempt status.

> ⊃ **Observation.** Sadly, some ministers and lay workers never fully repay a loan made to them by their church. The forgiveness of debt ordinarily represents taxable income to the debtor. As a result, if a church makes a loan to a minister or other staff member and the debt is later forgiven by the church, taxable income is generated in the amount of the forgiven debt.

13. Voluntary withholding. Compensation paid to ministers for services performed in the exercise of their ministry is not subject to either income tax or Social Security withholding. This is so whether ministers report their income taxes as employees or as self-employed. As a result, ministers are required to report and prepay their federal taxes by using the estimated tax procedure. This procedure requires ministers to estimate their income tax and self-employment tax liability for the year 2004 prior to April 15, 2004, and then to pay one-fourth of the total estimated tax liability on or by April 15, June 15, September 15, and the following January 15. These quarterly payments are accompanied by a "payment voucher" that is contained in IRS

Form 1040-ES. Some ministers find the estimated tax procedure inconvenient and undesirable (it is often hard to budget for the quarterly payments).

Ministers who report their income taxes as employees can enter into a voluntary withholding arrangement with their employing church. Under such an arrangement the employing church withholds income taxes as it would for any other employee, and also an additional amount for the minister's self-employment tax liability (otherwise the minister will need to use the estimated quarterly tax procedure to pay self-employment taxes). The additional amount withheld to cover self-employment taxes must be reported (on the minister's W-2 form and the church's 941 forms) as additional income tax withheld, and not as "Social Security taxes." A minister need only complete and submit to his or her church an IRS Form W-4 to begin voluntary withholding. The arrangement can be terminated by either the minister or the church at any time. Ministers who report their income taxes as self-employed could achieve the same benefit by entering into an unofficial withholding arrangement with their church under which the church withholds amounts from each paycheck to cover the minister's quarterly estimated tax payments. By each quarterly deadline, the church gives the minister the "withheld" compensation to assist him or her in making the quarterly payment. No W-4 should be prepared, since this would be evidence that the minister is in fact an employee. Churches should apprise ministers that they may enter into a voluntary withholding arrangement. For many ministers, such an arrangement will be preferable to the estimated tax procedure.

14. Special occasion gifts. It is common for ministers (and in some cases lay workers) to receive special occasion gifts during the course of the year. Examples include Christmas, birthday, and anniversary gifts. Churches and church staff members often do not understand how to report these payments for federal tax purposes. The general rule is this—if the "gifts" are funded through members' contributions to the church (i.e., the contributions are entered or recorded in the church's books as cash received and the members are given charitable contribution credit) then the distribution to the minister or lay worker should be reported as taxable compensation and included on his or her W-2 or 1099 and Form 1040. The same rule applies to special occasion "gifts" made to a minister or lay worker by the church out of the general fund. Members who contribute to special occasion offerings may deduct their contributions if (1) the contributions are to the church and are entered or recorded in the church's books as cash received, and (2) they are able to itemize deductions on Schedule A (Form 1040). Churches should be prepared to include such "gifts" to a minister or lay worker on his or her W-2 or 1099-MISC. Of course, members are free to make personal gifts to ministers and lay staff members, such as a card at Christmas accompanied by a check or cash. Such payments may be tax-free gifts to the recipient (though they are not deductible by the donor). These same rules apply to other kinds of special occasion gifts as well.

It is common for churches to make generous retirement gifts to retiring ministers (and in some cases lay workers). Do these gifts represent taxable income to the recipient? To the extent that the recipient is an employee (or would be classified as an employee by the IRS), there is no doubt that the "gift" would constitute taxable income. In 1986, section 102(c) was added to the Internal Revenue Code, which specifies that "any amount transferred by or for an employer to or for the benefit of an employee" shall not be excludable from gross income by the employee as a gift, other than certain employee achievement awards and insignificant holiday gifts. Those few ministers and lay workers who in fact are self-employed for income tax reporting purposes have some hope of having a retirement gift characterized as a tax-free gift rather than as taxable compensation for services rendered. Note however that such a conclusion is unlikely given the narrow definition of the term *gift*. The Supreme Court has noted that "a gift in the statutory sense . . . proceeds from a detached and disinterested generosity . . . out of affection, respect, admiration, charity, or like impulses . . . . The most critical consideration . . . is the transferor's intention." *Commissioner v. Duberstein, 363 U.S. 278, 285 (1960).* The Court also observed that "it doubtless is the exceptional payment by an employer to an employee that amounts to a gift," and that the church's characterization of the distribution as a "gift" is "not determinative—there must be an objective inquiry as to whether what is called a gift amounts to it in reality."

⊃ **Key point.** Intermediate sanctions, discussed earlier in this chapter, may apply to a retirement gift that results in unreasonable compensation to the recipient. Church leaders must be sure to consider this possibility before finalizing such a gift. If a retirement gift is excessive, the board members who authorized the gift may be assessed an excise tax equal to 10 percent of the amount by which the gift exceeds reasonable compensation (up to a maximum tax of $10,000, collectively). This is in addition to the excise taxes that may be assessed against the recipient.

15. Bargain sales. Occasionally, a church will sell property to a staff member at a price that is below market value. To illustrate, some churches "sell" a parsonage to a retiring minister at a price well below the property's fair market value. Other churches may sell a car or other church-owned vehicle to a minister at a below-market price. The important consideration with such "bargain sales" is this—the "bargain" element (i.e., the difference between the sales price charged by the church and the property's market value) must be reported as income to the minister on his or her W-2 or 1099-MISC and Form 1040. Churches should consider thoroughly the tax consequences of such sales before approving them.

16. Director immunity. Most states have adopted laws that provide *uncompensated* officers and directors of most charitable organizations (including churches) with limited immunity from legal liability. Congress enacted the Volunteer Protection Act in 1996 that provides similar protection as a matter of federal law. The immunity provided under state and federal law only applies to uncompensated officers and directors. What does this have to do with compensation planning? Simply this—churches should consider adopting an appropriate resolution clarifying that a minister's annual compensation package is for ministerial duties rendered to the church, *and is not for any duties on the church board.* Like any other church officer or director, the minister serves without compensation. Such a provision, if adopted, might qualify the minister for protection under the legal immunity law. It is worth considering.

17. Discretionary funds. It is a fairly common practice for a church to set aside a sum of money in a "discretionary fund" and give the senior minister the sole authority to distribute the money in the fund. In some cases, the minister has no instructions regarding permissible distributions. In other cases, the church establishes guidelines, but these often are oral and ambiguous. Many churches are unaware of the tax consequences of such arrangements. To the extent the minister has the authority to use any portion of the discretionary fund for his or her own personal use, then the entire fund must be reported as taxable income to the minister in the year it is funded. This is so even if the minister does not personally benefit from the fund. The mere fact that the minister *could* personally benefit from the fund is enough for the fund to constitute taxable income. The basis for this result is the "constructive receipt" rule, which is explained in the income tax regulations as follows:

> Income although not actually reduced to a taxpayer's possession is constructively received by him in the taxable year during which it is credited to his account, set apart for him, or otherwise made available so that he may draw upon it at any time, or so that he could have drawn upon it during the taxable year if notice of intention to withdraw had been given. However, income is not constructively received if the taxpayer's control of its receipt is subject to substantial limitations or restrictions.

For a discretionary fund to constitute taxable income to a minister, it is essential that the minister have the authority to "draw upon it at any time" for his or her own personal use. This means that the fund was established without any express prohibition against personal distributions. On the other hand, if a discretionary fund is set up by a board resolution that absolutely prohibits any distribution of the fund for the minister's personal use, then the constructive receipt rule is avoided. In the words of the regulation, "income is not constructively received if the taxpayer's control of its receipt is subject to substantial limitations or restrictions." Accordingly, in order to avoid the reporting of the entire discretionary fund as taxable income to the minister, it is essential that the fund be established by means of a board or congregational resolution that absolutely prohibits any use of the fund by the minister for personal purposes. Further, the resolution should specify that the fund may be distributed by the minister only for needs or projects that are consistent with the church's exempt purposes (as set forth in the church's charter). For accountability purposes, a member of the church board should review all distributions from the discretionary fund to be sure that these requirements are met.

18. Severance pay. Many churches have entered into severance pay arrangements with a pastor or other staff member. Such arrangements can occur when a pastor or staff member is dismissed, retires, or voluntarily resigns. Church treasurers must determine whether severance pay is taxable so that it can be properly reported (on a W-2 and the church's 941 forms). Also, taxes must be withheld from severance pay that is paid to nonminister employees (and ministers who have elected voluntary withholding). Failure to properly report severance pay can result in substantial penalties for both a church and the recipient.

In most cases severance pay represents taxable income to the recipient. There is one exception that will apply in some cases. The tax code excludes from taxable income "the amount of any damages received (whether by suit or agreement and whether as lump sums or as periodic payments) *on account of personal injuries or sickness.*" According to this provision, severance pay that is intended to settle personal injury claims may be nontaxable. The words "personal injuries" are defined broadly by the IRS and the courts, and include potential or threatened lawsuits based on discrimination and harassment.

⊃ **Key point.** The Tax Court has noted that "payments for terminating and canceling employment contracts are not payments for personal injuries."

Here are some factors to consider (based on actual cases) in deciding whether a severance payment made to a former worker represents taxable compensation or nontaxable damages in settlement of a personal injury claim: (1) An amount paid to a former employee "to reward her for her past services and to make her severance as amicable as possible" is taxable compensation. (2) An amount paid to a former employee under a severance agreement that contains no reference to a specific discrimination or other personal injury claim is taxable compensation. (3) If an employer pays a former employee severance pay, and reports the severance pay on a W-2 (or 1099), this is strong evidence that the amount represents taxable compensation. (4) If an employer continues one or more employee benefits (such as health insurance) as part of a severance agreement, this suggests that any amount payable under the agreement represents taxable compensation. (5) If an employer withholds taxes from amounts paid under a severance agreement, this "is a significant factor" in classifying the payments as taxable income. Of course, this factor will not be relevant in the case of ministers whose wages are not subject to withholding (unless they elect voluntary withholding). (6) Referring to a payment as "severance pay" indicates that it is taxable compensation rather than nontaxable damages in settlement of a personal injury claim. (7) Severance pay based on a former employee's salary (such as one year's salary) is more likely to be viewed as taxable compensation rather than nontaxable damages in settlement of a personal injury claim. (8) To be nontaxable, severance pay must represent "damages" received in settlement of a personal injury claim. The IRS has noted that this language requires more than a settlement agreement in which a former employee "waives" any discrimination or other personal injury claims he or she may have against an employer. If the employee "never filed a lawsuit or any other type of claim against [the employer] . . . the payment cannot be characterized as damages for personal injuries" since "there is no indication that personal injuries actually exist."

19. Income "splitting." Some ministers have attempted to "split" their church income with their spouse. This often is done to qualify the spouse for Social Security or other benefits or to avoid the Social Security "annual earnings test" (which reduces Social Security benefits to retired workers under 65 years of age who earn more than an amount prescribed by law). For income splitting arrangements to work, the courts have required proof that the spouse is in fact an employee of the church. This means that the spouse performs meaningful services on behalf of the church. The courts have pointed to a number of factors indicating that a spouse is *not* an employee: (1) The spouse did not receive a paycheck. (2) The spouse was not employed elsewhere. (3) The spouse's "compensation" was designed to provide a tax benefit (such as an IRA contribution), and lacked any economic reality. (4) Neither the church nor the minister documented any of the services the spouse performed. (5) Neither the church nor the minister could explain how the spouse's "salary" was determined. (6) There was no employment contract between the church and the minister's spouse. (7) No taxes were withheld from the spouse's "salary." (8) The spouse's income was not reported on the church's employment tax returns (Forms 941). (9) There was no evidence that wages were actually paid to the spouse, or that any employment contract existed, or that the spouse was treated as an employee.

The courts generally have been skeptical of attempts by taxpayers to shift income to a spouse. The message is clear—ministers should not attempt to obtain tax benefits by shifting income to a spouse unless there is economic reality to the arrangement.

Compensation Checklist For 2004

Item	Recommendations
salary	• avoid unreasonable compensation • avoid use of salary reductions that are not recognized by federal tax law
housing allowance	• for ministers who own or rent their home, designate a portion of their compensation as a housing allowance prior to December 31 for the next year • for ministers who live in a church-owned parsonage, designate a portion of their compensation as a parsonage allowance (if they will incur any housing expenses) prior to December 31 for the next year
equity allowance	• consider contributing to a tax-sheltered investment (such as a retirement fund) for ministers who live in church-owned parsonage, to compensate for their inability to accumulate equity in a home
accountable business expense reimbursement arrangement	• adopt an accountable business expense reimbursement arrangement by reimbursing only those business expenses that are adequately substantiated, and by requiring any excess reimbursements to be returned
travel expenses of a spouse	• reimburse a spouse's travel expenses incurred in accompanying a minister or lay employee on a business trip if the spouse's presence serves a legitimate business purpose and the expenses are duly substantiated (if these requirements are not met, then the church's reimbursements represent taxable income to the minister or lay employee)

church-owned vehicles	• avoid allowing minister or lay employee unrestricted personal use of a church-owned car (such usage must be valued and reported as taxable income) • consider adopting a policy limiting use of the car to business purposes and requiring it to be kept on church property (this avoids most recordkeeping requirements and does not result in any income to the minister) • an alternative is to limit use of the car to business purposes except for commuting to and from work (if the commuting is required for security reasons); each round trip commute represents $3 of reportable income
self-employment tax paid by church	• all ministers are self-employed for Social Security purposes with respect to their church work; this means they pay the self-employment tax rather than FICA taxes • some churches pay a portion of a minister's self-employment tax (as they pay a portion of a nonminister employee's FICA taxes); such payments represent taxable income • nonminister employees of churches that waived payment of FICA taxes by filing a timely Form 8274 are treated as self-employed for Social Security purposes—churches may want to pay a portion of the self-employment taxes owed by these workers if they do so for ministers
insurance	• consider paying health insurance premiums for ministers and lay employees (a tax-free fringe benefit for employees) • consider paying premiums for up to $50,000 of group term life insurance (a tax-free fringe benefit for employees)
retirement accounts	• consider contributing toward a tax-sheltered retirement plan
works made for hire	• urge staff members to write books and articles
qualified tuition reductions	• consider tuition discounts for ministers and lay employees whose children attend church-operated schools or preschools (they may be a tax-free fringe benefit)
loans to ministers	• avoid making any low or no interest loan to ministers • avoid making any loan to ministers at market rates unless permitted by state nonprofit corporation law
voluntary withholding	• ministers and lay workers who report their income taxes as employees should consider entering into a voluntary withholding arrangement wit the church (can avoid the quarterly estimated tax procedure); be sure to provide for the withholding of self-employment taxes too, but classify these extra withholdings as additional income taxes
special occasion gifts	• special occasion gifts to ministers and lay employees that are processed through the church's books, and for which contribution credit is given to donors, are taxable income to the minister or lay employee
bargain sales	• any property sold to a minister or lay employee at less than fair market value will result in taxable income (the amount by which the fair market value exceeds the sales price)

director immunity	• consider adopting a board resolution certifying that all church board members, including the senior minister, serve without compensation (this may qualify the minister for the limited immunity the law provides to uncompensated directors of nonprofit organizations)
discretionary funds	• avoid them unless (1) the minister cannot use the fund for his or her own personal use, (2) the fund may be distributed only for purposes consistent with the church's exempt purposes, and (3) a board member reviews all distributions to ensure compliance with these limits
severance pay	• severance pay is perfectly appropriate, but be sure that it is reported as additional taxable income unless it represents payment *on account of personal injuries or sickness*
income "splitting"	• do not attempt to shift a portion of a minister's compensation to his or her spouse for tax savings purposes, unless there is "economic reality" to the arrangement (the spouse performs services that otherwise would be compensated, and receives a reasonable rate of compensation)

Chapter 3

Using the Compensation Tables

The following chapters present compensation patterns for nine major positions within the local church. These profiles are the statistical heart of the *Compensation Handbook*. This chapter is designed to help you interpret the tables and maximize your use of the information in this book.

Each staff position has its own chapter including both compensation tables and a discussion of the findings. The tables are for full-time staff members, except for the last table in each chapter which provides data for part-time staff members. A comparative summary of all the positions is presented in Chapter 4.

Interpreting the Tables

Each chapter contains tables that portray compensation averages according to several key variables. The variables include the following:

- ☐ Church attendance (Sunday morning worship)
- ☐ Church income (from all sources)
- ☐ Attendance and setting[1]
- ☐ Gender
- ☐ Education
- ☐ Years employed (in current position)

Each table provides several columns of averages for the following compensation items:

- ☐ Salary—annual base salary
- ☐ Annual % Increase—the percent increase of base salary for the last year
- ☐ Parsonage—rental value of parsonage plus other housing expenses
- ☐ Housing—amount of housing allowance provided for the purchase or rent of a home and its up-keep and furnishings

---

1   Five settings are used: urban, suburban, medium size city, small town, rural. Each respondent was permitted to use his or her own judgment in defining their setting. The same approach is followed in using the tables. Each user must determine his or her own setting.

☐ Retirement—money church provides for retirement, not including social security payments

☐ Life Insurance—cost of life insurance provided for staff member as a benefit

☐ Health Insurance—cost of health insurance provided for staff member as a benefit

☐ Vacation/weeks—number of weeks of paid vacation

☐ Auto Allowance— the percentage of staff members receiving an auto allowance

☐ Education Funds—amount provided for continuing education

Immediately following the listing for the compensation item is a percentage. That percentage indicates the proportion of staff members who receive that benefit. For example, consider the following example taken from Chapter 5:

Table 5-3: Annual Compensation Of Senior Pastors By Church Setting And Size					
Attendance 0-250	**Urban**	**Suburban**	**Medium City**	**Small Town**	**Rural**
Number Of Respondents	52	141	105	161	54
Salary (100%*)	30,791	33,422	30,682	29,808	29,776
Annual % Increase (66%)	5%	5%	6%	6%	5%
Parsonage (19%)	11,702	15,421	13,419	8,557	13,017

Notice that (100%) follows *Salary*. This indicates that 100% of the respondents received a salary. In some tables, less than 100% of the respondents may receive a salary, indicating that they receive their compensation in other ways, For example, a pastor of a small church may receive his or her total compensation as a housing allowance and fringe benefits. Following *Parsonage* is (19%). This means that 19% of all senior pastors lived in a church provided parsonage. In the first column on the *Parsonage* line is the figure 11,702. This means that of the 19% of all senior pastors who received a parsonage allowance, those that serve urban churches with an attendance between 0-250 received on average an allowance of $11,702.

Total Compensation Comparisons

Below each table is a smaller box that lists the *average compensation* for each category. The *average compensation* includes the sum of the base salary, the housing or parsonage allowance, retirement contributions, life and health insurance payments, and educational funds. *This is the key figure for compensation analysis.* The following information is also found in the *Total Compensation Comparisons* box.

Standard Deviation

Following the average compensation is the standard deviation. The standard deviation is the most important and widely used measure of dispersion. In a normal distribution, one standard deviation away from the average represents 68.27% of all responses. For example, in this study the average compensation for pastors was $73,230. The standard deviation was $30,128. Thus, approximately 68% of all pastors receive a compensation falling between $43,102 (73,230 - 30,128) and $103,358 (73,230 + 30,128). A range of two standard deviations on either side of the average encompasses 95% of responses.

Median Income

Included in the *Total Compensation Comparisons* box is the median income for each reporting category. The median income represents the compensation amount below which 50% of the compensation totals fall. In essence, it divides the participants into two groups having equal frequency. For the purpose of this book, however, when the reporting category has an even number of participants, the median income that is reported is the compensation of the person representing N/2 (the total number of participants divided by two).

National Average

Included in the *Total Compensation Comparisons* box is the national average. This figure represents the average compensation nationwide for that position.

Rounding Errors

Rounding errors may exist in some of the data in this study. They do not, however, impact the final results in any significant way. Some of the hourly wages for part-time workers may deviate a few cents due to rounding errors.

Using the Tables To Plan Compensation

The most important use of this handbook is for compensation planning. The following example illustrates one approach of how this book can be used.

Example: Planning the Compensation of a Senior Pastor

> *Reverend West has served as senior pastor of Maywood Church for the past nine years. Maywood Church is a suburban congregation with an average Sunday worship attendance of 620, and an annual budget of $975,000. Reverend West has a Master of Divinity degree.*

The above example provides us with relevant data that can be used in coordination with the tables in this book. Church income is the single most important variable, followed by attendance, in predicting compensation. Other factors that we will use include the geographical setting of the church (in this case suburban), plus the pastor's length of service (nine years) and educational background (Master of Divinity degree).

> ⮂ **Key point.** The goal is not to come up with a single compensation number, but rather to identify a *base compensation range*. Once that range is determined, a variety of factors will affect the final choice of a specific level of compensation.

Step 1. The first step is to use the Tables in Chapter 5 to identify the *average base compensation range* for senior pastors in settings comparable to those of Reverend West. We begin by examining *church attendance* (Table 5-1), *church income* (Table 5-2), and *church attendance and geographical setting* (which for this example is Table 5-5: suburban churches with an attendance between 501-750). The main data we are interested in is found at the bottom of each table in the box labeled *Total Compensation Comparisons*. There we find data that summarizes the average church attendance, income, years employed, and compensation for the participants detailed in each column of each table. We also find the standard deviation for each column (for more information on standard deviations, see page 33). The relevant data from Tables 5-1, 5-2, and 5-5 are summarized below. In addition, the table below presents the average per capita giving.

1. Data for example	2. Average church attendance	3. Average church income	4. Average per capita giving	5. Average compensation	6. Standard deviation	7. Range based on one standard deviation (encompasses 68% of all respondents)
Maywood Church	620	$975,000	$1,573	to be determined		
Table 5-1 500-749	596	$1,062,332	$1,782	$86,323	$24,272	$62,051 - $110,595
Table 5-2 750-000 - 999,999	560	$867,566	$1,549	$80,338	$20,207	$60,131 - $100,545
Table 5-5 (Suburban)	638	$1,375,060	$2,155	$97,829	$24,729	$73,100 - 122,558

The above table enables us to establish two important compensation ranges. The first is based on the average compensation (column 5). The data from Tables 5-1, 5-2, and 5-5 provide us with a range of *average compensation* between $80,338 on the low end to $97,829 on the high end. These figures serve as an *average base compensation range*. The second important range is based on the standard deviation totals found in column 7. The *standard deviation range* indicates that 68% of pastors in similar settings have a compensation that falls between $60,131 on the low end to $122,558 on the high end. Going to the second standard deviation range could push the upper compensation amount to over $147,000 based on the data found in Table 5-5. Based on this data, we will begin by using the *average base compensation range* of $80,333 - $97,829. Other factors will then determine if that range should be modified.

Since church income is the most important factor in determining compensation, let's begin by focusing on column 3. First we see that the average church income for Table 5-5 is much higher than that for Maywood Church. This suggests that the average compensation for that group of $97,829 is probably on the high end for Maywood Church. Second, the income for Maywood Church is in between the averages found for the churches in Tables 5-1 and 5-2. However, in column 4 we note that the per capita giving for Maywood Church is very close to that of Table 5-2, but quite a bit below that of Table 5-1. On the other hand, Maywood Church has an attendance more similar to that of the churches found in Tables 5-1 and 5-5.

Based on the above observations we can make the following preliminary conclusions: (1) Maywood Church appears to be below average for the income data found in Table 5-5; (2) the per capita giving for Maywood Church is similar to that of Table 5-2; and (3) Maywood Church has a larger average attendance than the churches found in Table 5-1, but a lower per capita giving. These conclusions suggest that Maywood Church corresponds best to the data from Tables 5-1 and 5-2 which creates an average base compensation range of $80-338 - $86,323. Next, let's look at two variations of our example and the resulting implications for the base compensation range.

Variation 1. Suppose that Maywood Church has an income of $1,200,000 with the same attendance of 620. This produces a per capita giving of $1,935. The income and giving would then be higher than the averages from Tables 5-1 and 5-2, but still below that data from Table 5-5. That would suggest that Reverend West's *base compensation range* should be increased to approach the amount of $97,829 taken from Table 5-5. Furthermore, it may approach the upper limits of the first standard deviation boundary of Tables 5-1 and 5-2 which is between $100,545 - $110,595. It could even go into the next standard deviation boundary which is well over $130,000. That will depend on the factors that we examine in Steps 2-4.

Variation 2. Suppose that Maywood Church has an income of $800,000 and an attendance of 550 with a per capita income of $1,454 which are below the national averages presented above. That would suggest that

Reverend West's compensation may be lower than than the average range taken from column five. Yet, it would likely be above the national average of $73,230 based on the data from the Tables 5-1, 5-2, and 5-5. The final determination will depend on several of the factors that we examine below.

The next step is to determine if Reverend West's compensation range should be modified, and if so, by how much. The standard deviation range provides us with some working boundaries on both the upper and lower limits. It is likely that Reverend West will be above the national average of $73,230 since Maywood Church is larger than average, both in terms of size and income. In all likelihood, Reverend West's compensation will fall within the first standard deviation range found in Tables 5-1 and 5-2. If it does go higher it most likely will be based on the factors discussed in the remaining steps, such as education, length of service, and congregational values.

Step 2. The second step is to examine additional factors that might impact compensation such as *education* and *years of service*. This requires an examination of Table 5-9 (*Annual Compensation Of Senior Pastors by Education*) and Table 5-10 (*Annual Compensation of Senior Pastors by Years Employed*). These factors do not have as strong a correlation level with respect to compensation as do church income and attendance. As such, they are less useful in establishing a compensation range, but are helpful in deciding whether an individual is in the upper or lower parts of the range identified in Step 1.

1. Profile of Rev. West: M.Div. 9 years	2. Average church attendance	3. Average years of service	4. Average church income	5. Average per capita giving	6. Average compensation	7. Standard deviation	8. Range based on one standard deviation
Maywood Church	620	9	$975,000	$1,573	to be determined		
Table 5-9 Master	451	9	$658,521	$1,460	$71,195	$27,401	$43,7941 - $98,596
Table 5-10 6-10 years	555	8	$812,922	$1,464	74,038	$31,851	$42,187 - $105,889

In the *Total Compensation Comparisons* box of Table 5-9 we find that the average compensation for pastors with a master's degree is very close to the national average ($71,195 compared to $73,230). Similarly, those with 6-10 years of service, such as Pastor West, receive an annual compensation almost identical to the national average ($74,038 compared to $73,230). So, based on the data for Reverend West, no significant differential exists based on either education or years of service. However, in Tables 5-9 and 5-10 we note that the average church income and attendance are well below those of Maywood Church. As a result, the per capita giving represented in both tables is significantly below that of Maywood Church. At the same time we observe the standard deviation range exceeds $98,000 for both Tables 5-9 and 5-10 (see last column in table above). Based on our analysis from Step 1, we can conclude that Reverend West's compensation most likely will be well above the national average. While the proposed compensation range from Step 1 is higher than most other pastors with a similar level of education or years of service, it is only average for pastors in congregations of similar size or comparable income. Thus, we can conclude that the *base range* of $80,338 to $86,323, identified in Step 1, still remains applicable to Maywood Church and Reverend West, and based on church size and income, he is probably in the middle to higher end of that range. Remember, the *base range* is not the final range. Other factors may push the compensation to higher levels as noted in Step 3.

Variation 1. Suppose Pastor West has a doctoral degree. On average, Senior Pastors with a doctorate earn approximately $13,500 above the national average (see Table 5-9). In part this is because they serve larger churches with higher incomes. The average compensation for those with doctorates is $86,790. Again this fits within the broader scope of the range we identified from Step 1 ($80,338 to $86,323). The average church attendance for those with doctorates is 745, which is higher than Maywood Church's average of 620, and the average church income of $1,221,138 is higher than Maywood's $975,000. So all things considered, the compensation range from Step 1 still serves us fairly well. Nevertheless, a doctoral degree is a relevant factor that suggests higher levels of compensation are normal. How much higher will vary from one situation to another. In this case it would be a positive factor that might suggest moving toward or above the higher end of the range from Step 1 rather than the lower end of the range.

Variation 2. What if Reverend West's educational level is lower than a Master of Divinity degree? It would probably have little impact since the average attendance and income for pastors with lower levels of education are far below the averages of Maywood Church. The same would be true if Reverend West had served fewer years. In most cases, church income and attendance will be the strongest factors in determining overall compensation.

Step 3. The third step is to take into account the unique circumstances that define each individual situation. One factor is the cost of living for your area. Is it higher or lower than the national average? Your local Chamber of Commerce or a real estate agency can help you obtain that information. Other factors such as denominational affiliation (see Table 4-12), theological beliefs, pastoral performance, financial needs, goodwill, the local economy, personal motivation, congregational goals, internal church politics, and many other considerations will also contribute to the final decision. For some churches that may mean a final compensation package much lower or much higher than the projected range listed in Step 1. How that compensation will be divided up will vary greatly from one church to another, and even from one individual staff member to another. Care should be given, however, to avoid gender discrimination. This is a widespread problem involving many churches (see Table 4-8). In addition, a large disparity between the pastor's compensation, and that of other staff members, can have an impact on the rate of increase that the pastor may experience in future years. Often, once a staff member has reached the upper limits of his or her compensation range, future raises may be somewhat smaller in order to better compensate other staff members.

Step 4. The final step is to examine the *standard deviation* range for all senior pastors. Use Table 4-3 found in Chapter 4. That table indicates that the compensation of 95% of all pastors is less than $133,846 and that 68% of pastors earn less than $103,358. Thus, the final determination of Reverend West's compensation may significantly exceed the average range taken from column 4 of $80,338 to $86,323 without being unreasonable. Both tangible and intangible factors will impact the selection of the final compensation package. One concern is to make certain that the final compensation total does not fall so far outside of the normal distribution of clergy compensation that the church could possibly lose its tax exempt status due to payments that the tax court might consider "unreasonable" (see the discussion on *Salary* in Chapter 2). Naturally, those in the largest churches will have standard deviations that boost the upper limit above the $133,846 mark for two standard deviations. Appendix 5 graphically displays the standard deviation ranges of pastoral compensation based on church income.

The final determination of compensation is unique to every congregation. It would not be surprising to see a range of compensation for Reverend West somewhere between $80,000 - $100,000. Higher compensation levels are possible, and could be argued to be reasonable. It would be unlikely, however, for Reverend West to exceed $134,000, which would fall outside the limits of the second standard deviation range. Such a compensation level would require independent justification to avoid the possibility of intermediate sanctions (see Chapter 2 for a discussion of intermediate sanctions).

This same process can be used for each of the nine staff positions found in this handbook.

Chapter 4

Compensation Profiles: General Comparisons

This chapter provides comparisons of the average compensations for the nine staff positions included in this study. A summary table exists for each of the variables examined. More detailed analysis can be found in the individual chapter for each staff position.

As expected, pastors consistently rank first in total compensation for church staff members. Associate pastors received the second highest compensation amount followed generally by music and choir directors. The tables presented later in this chapter provide compensation rankings and comparisons according to the national averages for each position.

What factors determine compensation?

Church income, attendance, geographical setting, and the gender of the staff member were the four most important factors affecting total compensation. While no single factor played the decisive role, female staff members consistently received lower compensation than did their male counterparts.

Church income and attendance proved to be the most important variables affecting compensation for each of the nine positions examined in this study. Yet, the correlation between these variables and employee compensation accounts for only part of the variation in compensation amounts for these positions. These factors, while important, must be viewed in the context of other factors, the combination of which ultimately determine compensation. For example, theology may play a significant role in some churches in the determination of compensation. The compensation of a Catholic priest who has taken a vow of poverty will be low regardless of church size or income. In churches that promote financial prosperity as a sign of God's blessing, the pastor may receive a disproportionate amount of the church's total income. Politics and power may prove the decisive factors in determining compensation in a church embroiled in conflict. A building program may be the controlling factor somewhere else. In general, education, geographical setting, and years of service play some role in almost every church. Unfortunately, significant gender gaps existed for every position. While some of these gaps can be explained on the basis of demographic factors such as church setting or personal education, the conclusion cannot be escaped that gender discrimination is widespread within the church concerning compensation and the access to higher paying positions. The largest compensation gap between men and women was for church administrators—on average, for this position, females earned 63% of the compensation of males.

General Trends

This study examined the "rate of increase" with respect to compensation and church attendance, and compensation and church income. In this context, "rate of increase" refers to how fast compensation rose with respect to church attendance or size of church budget. For some staff positions, the rate of increase for total compensation was the highest for churches with an attendance between 300 and 750, while for other staff positions it was for church attendance above 750.

Church bookkeepers, secretaries, and custodians experienced only modest compensation growth increase as the church size increased. For these positions, compensation grows slowly regardless of church size. Some compensation growth appeared for larger churches, but even then, their total compensation was considerably less than the other church staff positions.

Similar trends could be seen based upon church income. Pastoral compensation increased at every budget level, but most dramatically once the church income exceeded $1,000,000. Associate pastors saw fairly steady increases as church income increased. CE directors, administrators, music directors, and youth ministers experienced only modest increases in compensation for budgets between $250,000 and $750,000. Bookkeepers, secretaries, and custodians did not fare as well. They experienced only modest increases as church income rose, with bookkeepers and custodians doing slightly better than secretaries.

Benefit Comparison

Benefits vary significantly from one position to the next. This was especially true for the more important benefits of health insurance and retirement programs. Only 33 to 80 percent of church staff have health insurance and fewer have retirement benefits. Bookkeepers, custodians, and secretaries are less likely to receive benefits than are the other professional staff members. Part-time staff members receive few fringe benefits. The tables below provide benefit comparisons (please note that some position titles and benefit listings have been abbreviated).

Table 4-1: Percentage of Full-time Staff Receiving Benefits

	Pastor	Associate	CE Dir.	Youth	Music	Admin.	Book.	Secretary	Custodian
raise	66%	73%	71%	71%	70%	72%	76%	64%	75%
parsonage	19%	8%	4%	9%	4%	2%	0%	0%	1%
housing	86%	89%	51%	66%	57%	22%	1%	0%	0%
retirement	70%	67%	58%	55%	59%	53%	41%	23%	40%
life ins.	36%	38%	39%	35%	36%	32%	35%	11%	32%
health ins.	77%	80%	76%	77%	76%	63%	60%	33%	62%
vacation	94%	93%	96%	95%	95%	92%	93%	87%	91%
education	50%	45%	41%	41%	39%	33%	15%	17%	6%
auto allow.	65%	89%	88%	89%	89%	84%	83%	29%	85%

Table 4-2: Percentage of Part-time Staff Receiving Benefits

	Pastor	Associate	CE Dir.	Youth	Music	Admin.	Book.	Secretary	Custodian
raise	33%	53%	59%	41%	58%	64%	64%	51%	53%
parsonage	12%	2%	0%	2%	0%	1%	0%	0%	0%
housing	67%	44%	9%	11%	2%	5%	0%	0%	0%
retirement	42%	22%	10%	9%	4%	17%	9%	5%	1%
life ins.	17%	10%	7%	0%	2%	7%	4%	1%	1%
health ins.	21%	31%	12%	5%	5%	18%	5%	5%	2%
vacation	67%	53%	55%	47%	43%	62%	42%	59%	32%
education	29%	20%	31%	20%	15%	20%	5%	8%	1%
auto allow.	50%	73%	74%	66%	65%	82%	75%	17%	57%

Note: the following tables are for comparative purposes only. For a full analysis of each staff position, consult chapters 5-13.

Table 4-3: National Church Staff Compensation Averages

Position	Average Compensation*	Standard Deviation	$\overline{X} \pm 1$ (68%)	$\overline{X} \pm 2$ (95%)
Pastor	73,230	30,128	43,102 - 103,358	12,974 - 133,486
Associate Pastor	59,742	19,943	39,799 - 79,685	19,856 - 99,628
Music Choir Dir.	56,875	19,354	37,521 - 76,229	18,167 - 95,583
Administrator	50,615	19,939	30,676 - 70,554	10,737 - 90,493
CE Director	50,313	17,403	32,910 - 67,716	15,507 - 85,116
Youth Minister	47,058	14,492	32,566 - 61,550	18,074 - 76,042
Bookkeeper	30,457	8,769	21,688 - 39,226	12,919 - 47,995
Custodian	29,047	10,260	18,787 - 39,307	8,527 - 49,567
Secretary	24,875	10,440	14,435 - 35,315	3,995 - 45,755

* The average compensation includes base salary, housing or parsonage allowance, retirement contribution, life and health insurance payments, and educational funds.

Using the Standard Deviation

In a normal distribution, one standard deviation away from the average represents 68.27% of all responses. For example, in this study the average compensation for pastors was $73,230. The standard deviation was $30,128. Thus, approximately 68% of all pastors receive a compensation falling between $43,102 (73,230 - 30,128) and $103,358 (73,230 + 30,128). A range of two standard deviations on either side of the average encompasses 95% of responses. The standard deviations listed in the table above apply only to national averages for each position and not to the other tables in this chapter.

Table 4-4: Annual Church Staff Compensation Averages By Church Attendance*

Attendance	0-99	100-299	300-499	500-749	750-999	over 1,000
Pastor	44,412	61,071	79,086	86,323	100,960	108,111
Associate Pastor	24,320	44,590	53,859	63,904	67,764	73,136
CE Director		32,799	43,805	48,317	54,177	59,753
Youth Minister	19,000	37,052	45,660	48,147	49,528	56,940
Music/Choir Dir.	17,223	42,177	51,209	57,094	56,953	68,207
Administrator	22,584	33,221	41,956	48,938	56,458	68,294
Bookkeeper		22,993	28,444	30,140	31,934	33,644
Secretary	19,537	22,755	24,733	26,424	27,861	30,264
Custodian	10,456	21,527	26,781	28,319	31,845	33,737

* The average compensation includes base salary, housing or parsonage allowance, retirement contribution, life and health insurance payments, and educational funds.

Table 4-5: Annual Church Staff Compensation Averages By Church Income*

Church Budget in $	0-249,999	250,000-499,999	500,000-749,000	750,000-999,999	1,000,000 +
Pastor	52,424	66,029	74,759	80,338	104,061
Associate Pastor	41,707	46,205	53,832	60,063	70,493
CE Director	32,141	32,933	40,845	44,683	56,699
Youth Minister	35,223	37,605	45,861	43,581	53,866
Music/Choir Dir.	41,043	40,432	49,155	52,215	63,542
Administrator	34,495	33,417	41,800	41,973	61,064
Bookkeeper	20,932	20,687	25,732	28,502	33,377
Secretary	20,155	24,052	26,242	26,917	29,633
Custodian	15,331	20,807	24,964	30,634	32,335

* The average compensation includes base salary, housing or parsonage allowance, retirement contribution, life and health insurance payments, and educational funds.

Table 4-6: Annual Church Staff Compensation Averages By Church Setting And Size*

Attendance Under 500	Urban	Suburban	Medium City	Small Town	Rural
Pastor	67,464	69,515	59,870	57,973	54,249
Associate Pastor	53,039	52,967	45,788	45,376	46,254
CE Director	40,965	43,686	36,184	37,634	
Youth Minister	44,907	43,118	36,216	42,767	37,480
Music/Choir Dir.	49,923	46,482	50,971	44,154	44,061
Administrator	43,103	37,574	35,095	31,250	38,132
Bookkeeper	33,893	26,571	28,771	20,631	31,605
Secretary	24,522	25,841	22,646	21,624	20,904
Custodian	26,562	28,451	21,592	19,019	21,997

* The average compensation includes base salary, housing or parsonage allowance, retirement contribution, life and health insurance payments, and educational funds.

Table 4-7: Annual Church Staff Compensation Averages By Church Setting And Size*

Attendance over 499	Urban	Suburban	Medium City	Small Town	Rural
Pastor	112,207	101,430	92,624	86,347	70,346
Associate Pastor	73,724	69,777	66,538	60,715	54,903
CE Director	62,259	54,934	55,178	51,052	42,253
Youth Minister	56,406	53,849	48,616	47,469	46,161
Music/Choir Dir.	64,852	63,687	60,084	57,181	45,934
Administrator	63,767	60,314	58,173	50,348	43,291
Bookkeeper	32,336	35,151	29,643	28,750	24,602
Secretary	30,643	29,232	26,903	24,453	25,066
Custodian	32,637	32,502	30,605	31,341	27,126

* The average compensation includes base salary, housing or parsonage allowance, retirement contribution, life and health insurance payments, and educational funds.

Table 4-8: Annual Church Staff Compensation Averages By Gender *

Gender	Male	Female	F/M Ratio
Pastor	73,814	55,046	75%
Associate Pastor	60,221	55,779	93%
CE Director	58,384	40,392	69%
Youth Minister	48,109	36,089	75%
Music/Choir Dir.	59,549	43,684	73%
Administrator	59,898	37,504	63%
Bookkeeper	34,882	30,173	87%
Secretary	25,170	24,855	99%
Custodian	30,652	20,684	67%

* The average compensation includes base salary, housing or parsonage allowance, retirement contribution, life and health insurance payments, and educational funds.

Table 4-9: Annual Church Staff Compensation Averages By Education*

Highest Degree	High School	Associate	Bachelor	Master	Doctorate
Pastor	63,818	56,148	64,758	71,195	86,790
Associate Pastor	52,473	45,411	53,313	63,075	68,379
CE Director	38,054	41,016	44,968	58,656	69,344
Youth Minister	43,044	43,852	44,574	53,486	51,406
Music/Choir Dir.	47,196	36,911	54,408	62,545	53,411
Administrator	40,829	44,752	50,792	59,758	57,304
Bookkeeper	28,602	30,887	32,378	30,896	
Secretary	23,962	24,885	25,801	26,427	24,599
Custodian	28,737	28,733	31,858	27,217	

* The average compensation includes base salary, housing or parsonage allowance, retirement contribution, life and health insurance payments, and educational funds.

Table 4-10: Annual Church Staff Compensation Averages By Years Employed*

Years Employed	0-5	6-10	11-15	over 15
Pastor	68,417	74,038	77,696	79,000
Associate Pastor	56,074	62,972	62,647	72,608
CE Director	46,931	54,150	53,589	61,535
Youth Minister	44,736	53,740	56,386	67,119
Music/Choir Dir.	53,767	57,887	56,557	67,341
Administrator	50,060	51,579	46,715	54,126
Bookkeeper	29,239	29,646	32,404	33,573
Secretary	22,280	24,500	25,000	26,450
Custodian	27,763	29,836	31,691	31,356

* The average compensation includes base salary, housing or parsonage allowance, retirement contribution, life and health insurance payments, and educational funds.

Table 4-11: Annual Hourly Compensation Averages For Part-Time Church Staff*

Hours per week	1-14	15-29	30-39	All Part-time
Pastor		27.02		35.31
Associate Pastor	19.49	15.78	26.43	17.70
CE Director	32.34	15.36	16.51	16.43
Youth Minister	16.02	14.03	14.17	13.57
Music/Choir Dir.	26.69	17.28	16.92	17.35
Administrator	16.89	17.16	18.46	17.29
Bookkeeper	11.76	12.27	15.88	11.79
Secretary	11.55	10.11	11.06	10.30
Custodian	12.50	9.67	10.13	9.96

* The average compensation includes base salary, housing or parsonage allowance, retirement contribution, life and health insurance payments, and educational funds.

Table 4-12: Denominational Compensation Comparisons*

	Pastor	As. Pastor	CE Dir.	Youth	Choir	Admin.	Book.	Sec.	Custodian
A/G (51/483) **	70,926	53,347	49,977	42,877	49,278	56,428	28,404	22,148	25,776
Baptist (206/601)	74,769	59,225	61,250	49,905	62,928	58,414	29,568	24,586	28,009
Catholic (11/1,659)	27,978					41,221		23,271	28,173
Christian (12/478)	62,266			45,537				24,972	
CMA (11/331)	63,465							27,873	
Ch of Christ (13/332)	63,747							26,488	
Ch of God (20/964)	84,380			46,307	52,523	57,950	34,782	23,793	31,782
Episcopal (29/308)	95,386	76,209		45,928	57,310	46,126	33,190	33,584	29,684
Evang. Free (27/646)	87,627	71,553	44,575	54,838	70,570	53,427		27,404	33,856
Independent (47/452)	71,489	58,344	54,297	49,677	60,324	48,636	27,895	24,706	35,157
Lutheran (72/380)	72,649	69,262	49,873	44,314	51,051	51,421		26,896	29,239
Mennonite (10/387)	63,726							23,460	
Nazarene (11/178)	52,031							20,533	
Nondenom. (121/870)	74,631	61,443	50,497	48,094	60,003	54,382	32,286	26,140	31,410
Pentecostal (10/158)	51,497							25,046	
Presbyterian (95/479)	83,970	66,293	46,445	47,776	54,384	48,014	35,051	25,539	28,561
UCC (30/223)	64,954				42,644	35,861		24,684	
United Meth. (78/477)	81,322	56,473	39,194	40,382	51,476	44,997	31,420	24,126	24,809
Other*** (177/446)	64,596	52,585	47,215	44,788	52,196	46,004	28,915	23,081	30,687
National (886/571)	73,230	59,742	50,313	47,058	56,875	50,615	30,457	24,875	29,047

* The average compensation includes base salary, housing or parsonage allowance, retirement contribution, life and health insurance payments, and educational funds.

** The first number in parentheses following the denominational listing indicates the number of senior pastors reporting from that denomination. The second number is the average Sunday morning worship attendance for that denominational group. Blank spaces in the columns for other staff members indicates less than 10 respondents. Refer to "Other" at the bottom of the table.

*** Includes all other denominations with less than 10 respondents..

Chapter 5

Senior Pastors

Employment Profile

Senior pastors provided a significant number of responses to this survey with 1,053 participants. This group was composed of both pastors who oversee a multiple staff including other clergy and individual pastors who are the only ordained employee of their church. As can be expected, this group is quite diverse. Significant differences exist in training, church size, church income, and years served. Approximately 98% of the pastors surveyed serve full-time. The following statistical features profile this sample:

	Full-time	Part-time
❑ Number of Respondents	1,029	24
❑ Ordained	99%	100%
❑ Average years employed	10	6
❑ Male	97%	92%
❑ Female	3%	8%
❑ Self-employed	6%	36%
❑ Church Employee	94%	64%
❑ Senior pastor of multiple staff	80%	50%
❑ Solo pastor	20%	50%
❑ High School Diploma	3%	12%
❑ Associate Degree	1%	0%
❑ Bachelor Degree	19%	12%
❑ Master Degree	49%	29%
❑ Doctorate	28%	47%

Compensation Analysis

The analysis below is based upon the tables found later in this chapter. The tables present compensation data for pastors who serve full-time according to church attendance, church income, combinations of size and setting, gender, education, and years employed. The final table provides data for part-time pastors based upon the number of hours worked. In this way, the pastor's compensation can be analyzed and compared from a variety of useful perspectives. The total compensation amount includes the base salary, housing or parsonage amount, retirement contribution, life and health insurance payments, and educational funds.

Key Points

✎ *Church income had the strongest correlation with compensation.* While, the correlation is a fairly strong one, it should be considered as only one of many factors that determined compensation. As the church's income increased, compensation went up. Pastors in churches with budgets over $600,000 tended to be equal to or above the national average compensation. Pastors serving churches with incomes over $1,000,000 received on average almost twice the compensation of a pastor in a church with a budget under $250,000. *See Table 5-2.*

✎ *Church attendance affected pastoral compensation.* Of the pastors surveyed, approximately 50% worked in churches with an average attendance under 300 people. The compensation of these pastors was below the national average. Compensation increases significantly as attendance moves between 200 to 300. The average number of years served tends to increase as attendance increases. *See Table 5-1.*

✎ *A church's geographical setting affected pastoral compensation.* Generally, pastors of suburban and urban churches have the highest compensation. Historically, urban pastors have the highest levels of compensation for larger churches. Churches located in urban, suburban and medium size cities tended to provide higher housing allowances, retirement contributions, and insurance payments, although health insurance payments are often comparable. *See Tables 5-3, 5-4, 5-5, 5-6 and 5-7.*

✎ *Gender disparities existed concerning pastoral compensation.* On average, female pastors earn less than their male counterparts, but the gap has declined somewhat over the past decade. At this time, women do not have access to larger churches. The average congregational size that men serve is about 500 people, while for women it is under 200. The difference in congregational size represents a considerable difference in church income which impacts the overall compensation. *See Table 5-8.*

✎ *A relationship existed between educational achievement and income for pastors.* Pastors with a high school diploma earned approximately $7,400 less than pastors with a master's degree. In general, only those groups with graduate degrees reached the national average. The biggest increase in compensation occurred when a pastor obtained a doctoral degree. These individuals were more likely to serve larger urban or suburban churches which provided the highest levels of compensation. Average years employed was similar regardless of educational background. Over 90% of the respondents were college graduates and 75% had graduate degrees. The most common was a master's degree held by 48% of those responding to this survey. Over 27% held doctoral degrees. *See Table 5-9.*

✎ *Years of service had an impact on compensation.* Those serving for less than five years in their current position (39% of the respondents) received about $10,500 a year less in total compensation than those who had served over 15 years. The difference, however, appears to be more dependent on church income than on years served. Those serving the longest tended to be in bigger churches with significantly higher incomes. *See Table 5-10.*

✎ **On average, part-time pastors worked 18 hours per week for their church.** Most part-time pastors served churches with an average attendance under 150 people. Their tenure was less frequent than that of full-time pastors. Comparatively, compensation was significantly less for part-time pastors than those serving full-time. *See Table 5-11.*

Benefit Analysis

Full-time staff members. The pastor was the most highly paid position in the local church and received the best benefits. Most pastors own or rent a home. Slightly over three-fourths of pastors received health insurance and 70% had retirement benefits.

Part-time staff members. Approximately 2% of the pastors in this survey served their church on a part-time basis. Part-time pastors received fewer benefits than full-time pastors in every compensation category.

Benefits	Full-time	Part-time
☐ Housing allowance	86%	67%
☐ Parsonage provided	19%	12%
☐ Retirement	70%	42%
☐ Health insurance	77%	21%
☐ Life insurance	36%	17%
☐ Paid vacation	94%	67%
☐ Auto allowance	80%	50%
☐ Continuing education expenses	50%	29%

Eleven Year Compensation Trend: National Averages for Pastors

1993	$49,536	1999	$62,869
1994	$50,400	2000	$66,096
1995	$51,592	2001	$69,543
1996	$55,027	2002	$71,232
1997	$56,172	2003	$73,230
1998	$59,067		

Table 5-1: Annual Compensation Of Senior Pastor By Worship Attendance

Church Attendance	0-99	100-299	300-499	500-749	750-999	1,000+
Number Of Respondents	121	399	167	134	70	106
Salary (100%)	23,286	33,541	43,342	47,000	59,218	64,260
Annual % Increase (66%)	6%	5%	6%	5%	4%	5%
Parsonage (19%)	11,121	11,917	17,480	18,622	19,050	23,248
Housing (86%)	14,424	18,181	23,390	25,720	27,741	30,434
Retirement (70%)	4,319	4,865	5,494	6,656	6,804	6,771
Life Insurance (36%)	984	762	1,319	2,029	1,139	1,476
Health Insurance (77%)	6,427	7,336	8,627	8,702	8,319	8,095
Vacation/weeks (94%)	3	3	4	4	4	4
Education Funds (50%)	1,143	1,246	1,585	1,817	1,760	2,326
Receive Auto Allow. (80%)	61%	73%	91%	90%	91%	91%

* The percentage following each compensation item indicates the portion of all senior pastors who received that form of compensation. The averages in each column are for those individuals who actually received that compensation item. See Chapter 3 for a full explanation of how to read this table.

Total Compensation Comparisons

Church Attendance	0-99	100-299	300-499	500-749	750-999	1,000+
Average attendance	67	178	373	596	851	2,357
Average church income	118,516	283,721	704,216	1,062,332	1,670,420	2,763,135
Average years employed	8	8	10	12	11	13
Average compensation*	44,412	61,071	79,086	86,323	100,960	108,111
Standard deviation	17,350	17,648	22,857	24,272	26,253	40,304
Median compensation	44,150	59,337	76,564	85,524	97,950	105,560

National average: $73,230 with a standard deviation of $30,128 (see Chapter 4, Table 4-3).

Total respondents: 997

* includes base salary, housing or parsonage allowance, retirement contribution, life and health insurance payments, and educational funds.

Table 5-2: Annual Compensation Of Senior Pastor By Church Income

Church Income in $	0-249,999	250,000-499,999	500,000-749,000	750,000-999,999	1,000,000 +
Number Of Respondents	296	216	110	81	233
Salary (100%)	28,797	35,550	41,428	42,138	59,970
Annual % Increase (66%)	5%	5%	6%	4%	5%
Parsonage (19%)	11,442	12,958	18,573	20,343	24,012
Housing (86%)	15,020	19,722	23,065	25,154	29,090
Retirement (70%)	4,602	5,051	4,926	5,348	7,262
Life Insurance (36%)	815	905	1,287	1,118	1,776
Health Insurance (77%)	7,024	7,539	8,047	8,607	8,609
Vacation/weeks (94%)	3	4	4	4	4
Education Funds (50%)	1,113	1,266	1,627	1,481	2,188
Receive Auto Allow. (80%)	65%	80%	87%	93%	93%

* The percentage following each compensation item indicates the portion of all senior pastors who received that form of compensation. The averages in each column are for those individuals who actually received that compensation item. See Chapter 3 for a full explanation of how to read this table.

Total Compensation Comparisons

Church Income	0-249,999	250,000-499,999	500,000-749,999	750,000-999,999	1,000,000+
Average attendance	143	243	390	560	1,392
Average church income	150,188	346,307	606,270	867,566	2,104,268
Average years employed	9	8	10	12	12
Average compensation*	52,424	66,029	74,759	80,338	104,061
Standard deviation	18,873	20,872	17,051	20,207	31,437
Median compensation	50,802	63,956	72,183	76,564	99,740

National average: $73,230 with a standard deviation of $30,128 (see Chapter 4, Table 4-3).

Total respondents: 936

* includes base salary, housing or parsonage allowance, retirement contribution, life and health insurance payments, and educational funds.

Table 5-3: Annual Compensation Of Senior Pastor By Church Setting And Size

Attendance 0-250	Urban	Suburban	Medium City	Small Town	Rural
Number Of Respondents	52	141	105	161	54
Salary (100%)	30,791	33,422	30,682	29,808	29,776
Annual % Increase (66%)	5%	5%	6%	6%	5%
Parsonage (19%)	11,702	15,421	13,419	8,557	13,017
Housing (86%)	20,915	20,265	18,750	14,452	11,976
Retirement (70%)	6,770	4,891	4,326	4,559	4,407
Life Insurance (36%)	708	908	606	1,007	633
Health Insurance (77%)	7,720	7,990	6,609	6,745	6,426
Vacation/weeks (94%)	4	4	3	3	3
Education Funds (50%)	1,279	1,465	1,477	1,061	988
Receive Auto Allow. (80%)	81%	80%	70%	62%	56%

* The percentage following each compensation item indicates the portion of all senior pastors who received that form of compensation. The averages in each column are for those individuals who actually received that compensation item. See Chapter 3 for a full explanation of how to read this table.

Total Compensation Comparisons

Church Size: 0-250	Urban	Suburban	Medium City	Small Town	Rural
Average attendance	142	153	149	139	136
Average church income	260,562	279,600	278,984	193,472	206,129
Average years employed	8	8	9	8	8
Average compensation*	61,806	64,126	57,091	52,239	51,245
Standard deviation	27,287	18,983	16,247	18,934	15,499
Median compensation	56,777	62,450	57,130	53,077	51,500

National average: $73,230 with a standard deviation of $30,128 (see Chapter 4, Table 4-3).

Total respondents: 513

* includes base salary, housing or parsonage allowance, retirement contribution, life and health insurance payments, and educational funds.

Table 5-4: Annual Compensation Of Senior Pastor By Church Setting And Size

Attendance 251-500	Urban	Suburban	Medium City	Small Town	Rural
Number Of Respondents	18	90	41	59	9
Salary (100%)	46,666	42,929	39,415	44,003	38,107
Annual % Increase (66%)	4%	5%	7%	5%	7%
Parsonage (19%)	20,000	20,134	9,827	15,369	9,000
Housing (86%)	30,031	24,674	21,077	20,155	26,080
Retirement (70%)	8,336	5,288	5,982	4,578	5,873
Life Insurance (36%)	8,981	487	1,739	1,123	646
Health Insurance (77%)	8,662	8,515	8,829	8,592	8,420
Vacation/weeks (94%)	4	4	4	4	4
Education Funds (50%)	2,342	1,588	1,170	1,462	1,167
Receive Auto Allow. (80%)	100%	93%	85%	86%	89%

* The percentage following each compensation item indicates the portion of all senior pastors who received that form of compensation. The averages in each column are for those individuals who actually received that compensation item. See Chapter 3 for a full explanation of how to read this table.

Total Compensation Comparisons

Church Size: 251-500	Urban	Suburban	Medium City	Small Town	Rural
Average attendance	394	374	369	359	361
Average church income	985,530	682,416	670,835	589,390	518,426
Average years employed	11	11	9	11	12
Average compensation*	96,725	79,992	70,645	75,239	72,000
Standard deviation	32,615	17,093	20,101	25,419	14,136
Median compensation	89,500	76,564	68,988	70,650	69,000

National average: $73,230 with a standard deviation of $30,128 (see Chapter 4, Table 4-3).

Total respondents: 217

* includes base salary, housing or parsonage allowance, retirement contribution, life and health insurance payments, and educational funds.

Table 5-5: Annual Compensation Of Senior Pastor By Church Setting And Size

Attendance 501-750	Urban	Suburban	Medium City	Small Town	Rural
Number Of Respondents	18	45	29	22	7
Salary (100%)	54,035	52,173	44,229	45,776	38,958
Annual % Increase (66%)	6%	4%	4%	7%	16%
Parsonage (19%)	34,934	21,048	10,800	2,550	11,500
Housing (86%)	28,512	29,100	25,890	24,350	20,429
Retirement (70%)	10,510	7,411	5,592	6,069	3,872
Life Insurance (36%)	726	2,028	583	539	50
Health Insurance (77%)	10,100	9,060	7,868	9,865	6,638
Vacation/weeks (94%)	4	4	4	4	4
Education Funds (50%)	2,312	1,726	1,442	2,431	2,083
Receive Auto Allow. (80%)	63%	93%	90%	86%	100%

* The percentage following each compensation item indicates the portion of all senior pastors who received that form of compensation. The averages in each column are for those individuals who actually received that compensation item. See Chapter 3 for a full explanation of how to read this table.

Total Compensation Comparisons

Church Size: 501-750	Urban	Suburban	Medium City	Small Town	Rural
Average attendance	634	638	624	614	595
Average church income	1,410,310	1,375,060	936,139	1,024,247	747,714
Average years employed	10	12	10	11	11
Average compensation*	104,329	97,829	79,876	81,417	63,189
Standard deviation	23,691	24,729	21,978	24,619	13,605
Median compensation	99,900	91,464	76,440	81,737	66,472

National average: $73,230 with a standard deviation of $30,128 (see Chapter 4, Table 4-3).

Total respondents: 121

* includes base salary, housing or parsonage allowance, retirement contribution, life and health insurance payments, and educational funds.

Table 5-6: Annual Compensation Of Senior Pastor By Church Setting And Size

Attendance 751-1,000	Urban	Suburban	Medium City	Small Town	Rural
Number Of Respondents	8	32	21	5	3
Salary (100%)	71,895	58,018	51,728	70,576	47,884
Annual % Increase (66%)	2%	4%	4%	4%	4%
Parsonage (19%)	18,000	8,500	24,100	0	0
Housing (86%)	24,630	26,551	27,278	27,473	31,092
Retirement (70%)	6,085	6,335	5,862	4,892	5,133
Life Insurance (36%)	372	1,620	871	170	216
Health Insurance (77%)	9,703	8,025	8,512	6,411	8,065
Vacation/weeks (94%)	4	4	4	4	3
Education Funds (50%)	1,750	1,597	1,830	1,000	1,000
Receive Auto Allow. (80%)	88%	88%	90%	100%	100%

* The percentage following each compensation item indicates the portion of all senior pastors who received that form of compensation. The averages in each column are for those individuals who actually received that compensation item. See Chapter 3 for a full explanation of how to read this table.

Total Compensation Comparisons

Church Size: 751-1000	Urban	Suburban	Medium Town	Small Town	Rural
Average attendance	910	882	885	826	933
Average church income	1,917,591	1,610,241	1,562,205	1,531,097	1,768,852
Average years employed	8	11	12	17	5
Average compensation*	113,604	97,169	95,131	104,263	92,985
Standard deviation	27,328	22,173	23,147	44,464	14,222
Median compensation	101,210	95,758	87,211	83,305	76,643

National average: $73,230 with a standard deviation of $30,128 (see Chapter 4, Table 4-3).

Total respondents: 69

* includes base salary, housing or parsonage allowance, retirement contribution, life and health insurance payments, and educational funds.

Table 5-7: Annual Compensation Of Senior Pastor By Church Setting And Size

Attendance Over 1,000	Urban	Suburban	Medium City	Small Town	Rural
Number Of Respondents	16	41	28	10	2
Salary (100%)	72,001	68,126	61,615	59,522	38,250
Annual % Increase (66%)	5%	6%	5%	5%	9%
Parsonage (19%)	35,667	20,142	25,680	0	8,000
Housing (86%)	34,255	30,826	31,497	23,946	17,004
Retirement (70%)	8,478	7,435	5,999	6,772	0
Life Insurance (36%)	3,182	997	2,126	720	0
Health Insurance (77%)	7,849	8,984	7,251	5,777	10,088
Vacation/weeks (94%)	4	4	4	4	4
Education Funds (50%)	912	3,534	2,080	1,970	1,200
Receive Auto Allow. (80%)	88%	93%	89%	90%	100%

* The percentage following each compensation item indicates the portion of all senior pastors who received that form of compensation. The averages in each column are for those individuals who actually received that compensation item. See Chapter 3 for a full explanation of how to read this table.

Total Compensation Comparisons

Church Size: 1,000 +	Urban	Suburban	Medium City	Small Town	Rural
Average attendance	3,903	2,587	2,000	1,289	1,750
Average church income	3,678,022	3,380,088	2,124,264	1,988,992	804,592
Average years employed	16	13	12	17	6
Average compensation*	117,512	113,770	107,393	93,107	61,440
Standard deviation	70,370	30,721	30,045	39,100	14,297
Median compensation	112,156	105,560	104,223	81,176	

National average: $73,230 with a standard deviation of $30,128 (see Chapter 4, Table 4-3).

Total respondents: 97

* includes base salary, housing or parsonage allowance, retirement contribution, life and health insurance payments, and educational funds.

Table 5-8: Annual Compensation Of Senior Pastor By Gender

Gender	Male	Female
Number Of Respondents	997	32
Salary (100%)	41,154	26,566
Annual % Increase (66%)	5%	3%
Parsonage (19%)	13,985	12,440
Housing (86%)	21,963	18,908
Retirement (70%)	5,607	5,013
Life Insurance (36%)	1,208	1,117
Health Insurance (77%)	7,903	6,283
Vacation/weeks (94%)	4	4
Education Funds (50%)	1,562	985
Receive Auto Allow. (80%)	81%	62%

* The percentage following each compensation item indicates the portion of all senior pastors who received that form of compensation. The averages in each column are for those individuals who actually received that compensation item. See Chapter 3 for a full explanation of how to read this table.

Total Compensation Comparisons

Gender	Male	Female
Average attendance	543	168
Average church income	816,600	202,034
Average years employed	10	6
Average compensation*	73,814	55,046
Standard deviation	30,196	21,270
Median compensation	69,691	50,802

National average: $73,230 with a standard deviation of $30,128 (see Chapter 4, Table 4-3).

Total respondents: 1,029

* includes base salary, housing or parsonage allowance, retirement contribution, life and health insurance payments, and educational funds.

Table 5-9: Annual Compensation Of Senior Pastor By Education

Highest Degree	High School	Associate	Bachelor	Master	Doctorate
Number Of Respondents	31	10	175	432	251
Salary (100%)	35,554	27,636	36,016	38,832	49,580
Annual % Increase (66%)	7%	5%	6%	5%	5%
Parsonage (19%)	14,737	13,867	9,275	13,685	19,084
Housing (86%)	20,621	18,585	20,943	20,791	24,494
Retirement (70%)	6,755	4,425	4,185	5,599	6,404
Life Insurance (36%)	882	1,531	1,256	1,023	1,657
Health Insurance (77%)	6,515	6,156	7,168	8,020	8,452
Vacation/weeks (94%)	4	3	3	4	4
Education Funds (50%)	2,039	500	1,528	1,465	1,608
Receive Auto Allow. (80%)	77%	90%	78%	80%	82%

* The percentage following each compensation item indicates the portion of all senior pastors who received that form of compensation. The averages in each column are for those individuals who actually received that compensation item. See Chapter 3 for a full explanation of how to read this table.

Total Compensation Comparisons

Highest Degree	High School	Associate	Bachelor	Masters	Doctorate
Average attendance	362	237	522	451	745
Average church income	625,941	521,735	645,921	658,521	1,221,138
Average years employed	12	12	10	9	10
Average compensation*	63,818	56,148	64,758	71,195	86,790
Standard deviation	37,594	22,076	26,237	27,401	32,796
Median compensation	56,220	57,125	60,700	67,620	82,000

National average: $73,230 with a standard deviation of $30,128 (see Chapter 4, Table 4-3).

Total respondents: 899

* includes base salary, housing or parsonage allowance, retirement contribution, life and health insurance payments, and educational funds.

Table 5-10: Annual Compensation Of Senior Pastor By Years Employed

Years Employed	0-5	6-10	11-15	over 15
Number Of Respondents	398	249	147	218
Salary (100%)	37,406	40,734	44,083	44,403
Annual % Increase (66%)	5%	6%	6%	4%
Parsonage (19%)	11,992	15,579	13,725	17,661
Housing (86%)	21,093	22,074	22,337	23,011
Retirement (70%)	5,890	5,272	4,823	5,937
Life Insurance (36%)	1,112	1,131	1,509	1,216
Health Insurance (77%)	7,799	7,748	7,953	8,010
Vacation/weeks (94%)	3	4	4	4
Education Funds (50%)	1,423	1,837	1,302	1,586
Receive Auto Allow. (80%)	75%	83%	84%	83%

* The percentage following each compensation item indicates the portion of all senior pastors who received that form of compensation. The averages in each column are for those individuals who actually received that compensation item. See Chapter 3 for a full explanation of how to read this table.

Total Compensation Comparisons

Years Employed	0-5	6-10	11-15	Over 15
Average attendance	407	555	562	721
Average church income	597,496	812,922	933,934	1,045,884
Average years employed	3	8	13	22
Average compensation*	68,417	74,038	77,696	79,000
Standard deviation	26,362	31,851	32,594	31,511
Median compensation	64,223	70,650	73,056	74,910

National average: $73,230 with a standard deviation of $30,128 (see Chapter 4, Table 4-3).

Total respondents: 1,012

* includes base salary, housing or parsonage allowance, retirement contribution, life and health insurance payments, and educational funds.

Table 5-11: Annual Compensation Of Part-Time Senior Pastors By Hours Worked

Hours Per Week	1-14	15-29	30-39	All Part-time
Number of Respondents	0	6	0	24
Salary (100%)		16,350		20,449
Annual % Increase (33%)		5%		4%
Parsonage (12%)		10,400		13,600
Housing (67%)		12,267		10,969
Retirement (42%)		2,860		3,642
Life Insurance (17%)		50		4,731
Health Insurance (21%)		8,646		5,054
Vacation/weeks (67%)		2		3
Education Funds (29%)		600		907
Receive Auto Allow. (50%)		100%		50%

* The percentage following each compensation item indicates the portion of all part-time senior pastors who received that form of compensation. The averages in each column are for those individuals who actually received that compensation item. See Chapter 3 for a full explanation of how to read this table.

Total Compensation Comparisons

Hours Per Week	1-14	15-29	30-39	All Part-time
Average attendance		185		137
Average church income		260,632		200,741
Average years employed		8		6
Average hours per week		21		18
Average compensation		29,506		33,085
Ave. hourly compensation*		27.02		35.31
Ave. hourly salary**		14.97		21.85

Total respondents: 24

* includes base salary, housing or parsonage allowance, retirement contribution, life and health insurance payments, and educational funds.

** includes base salary only; see discussion on "rounding errors" in Chapter 3.

Chapter 6

Associate Pastors

Employment Profile

The roles and duties of the associate pastor are quite diverse depending upon the church. Associate pastors receive approximately the same benefits as senior pastors, but the total compensation amounts are considerably less. On average, associate pastors tend to receive a compensation of about 75-80% of that of pastors. The gap widens even more once church attendance exceeds 1,000 or church income passes $1,000,000. The statistical profile of associate pastors was as follows:

	Full-time	Part-time
☐ Number of Respondents	427	59
☐ Ordained	95%	83%
☐ Male	89%	71%
☐ Female	11%	29%
☐ Years employed	7	5
☐ Self-employed	2%	9%
☐ Church Employee	98%	91%
☐ High School Diploma	5%	9%
☐ Associate Degree	1%	4%
☐ Bachelor Degree	28%	33%
☐ Master Degree	55%	50%
☐ Doctorate	11%	4%

Compensation Analysis

The analysis below is based upon the tables found later in this chapter. The tables present compensation data for associate pastors who serve full-time according to worship attendance, church income, combinations of size and setting, gender, education, and years employed. The final table provides data for part-time pastors based upon the number of hours worked. In this way, the associate pastor's compensation can be analyzed and compared from a variety of useful perspectives. The total compensation amount includes the base salary, housing or parsonage allowance, retirement contribution, life and health insurance payments, and educational funds.

Key Points

✎ *Church worship attendance had a direct influence upon the compensation of the associate pastor.* Associate pastors in churches with an average attendance under 500 were below the national average; others were above. The value of several fringe benefits also tended to increase with church size. *See Table 6-1.*

✎ *Church income impacted the compensation of associate pastors.* Church income is the most important factor affecting total compensation, although many factors play a role. Over 40% of the associate pastors served in churches with an average annual budget over $1,000,000. Housing allowance amount increased with church income. Total compensation did not reach the national average until the church's annual income reached approached $900,000 per year. *See Table 6-2.*

✎ *A church's geographic setting impacted the compensation of associate pastors.* In general, associate pastors serving churches located in suburban, urban and medium size cities received the highest average compensation. Generally, urban churches tended to have the highest church income. Individuals serving in rural churches received the lowest average compensation. *See Tables 6-3, 6-4, 6-5, 6-6, and 6-7.*

✎ *Female associate pastors received lower levels of compensation than did their male counterparts.* On average, females earned 92% of the compensation of their male counterparts, the same as the last two years, but up from 87% in 2000. The difference in total compensation was $4,500 this year, up from $3,600 last year. Men tended to serve in much larger churches with budgets averaging far more than those churches in which females served. That church income difference may account for a significant part of the compensation differential. *See Table 6-8.*

✎ *College graduates earned more than nongraduates, but the highest compensation levels were found with those having graduate degrees.* Sixty-six percent of this sample had graduate degrees. These individuals received higher levels of compensations than those with less education. They tended to work in urban or suburban churches which generally had significantly higher income than other churches. Associate pastors with a bachelor's degree earned about the same as those with a high school diploma (although that gap differs widely from one year to the next). Both, however, were below the national average. *See Table 6-9.*

✎ *Total compensation was partially tied to length of service.* Compensation increased with length of service. Those serving the longest tended to serve in churches with average annual incomes over $2,000,000. In general, church income is more significant than years served on final compensation amounts, although, in this sample, those with 21 years of service earned significantly more than the other groups. *See Table 6-10.*

✎ *Most part-time associate pastors work about half-time at the church.* The average annual compensation for these part-time associates is about 31% of their full-time counterparts. *See Table 6-11.*

Benefit Analysis

Full-time staff members. Full-time associate pastors received benefit packages commensurate with those of senior pastors. Senior pastors were more likely to live in a church owned parsonage than were associates, although about the same percentage from both groups had a housing allowance as part of their compensation. For a comparative analysis of all staff positions, see Table 4-1 in Chapter 4.

Part-time staff members. About 12% percent of the associate pastors participating in this survey worked at their church on a part-time basis. Salary and benefits were tied to the number of hours employed.

Benefits	Full-time	Part-time
❒ Housing allowance	89%	44%
❒ Parsonage provided	8%	2%
❒ Retirement contributions	67%	22%
❒ Life insurance	38%	10%
❒ Health insurance	80%	31%
❒ Paid vacation	93%	53%
❒ Auto allowance	89%	73%
❒ Continuing education funds	45%	20%

Eleven Year Compensation Trend: National Averages for Associate Pastors

❒	1993	$39,970
❒	1994	$41,109
❒	1995	$44,058
❒	1996	$44,710
❒	1997	$45,042
❒	1998	$47,076
❒	1999	$49,827
❒	2000	$51,973
❒	2001	$54,729
❒	2002	$58,072
❒	2003	$59,742

Table 6-1: Annual Compensation Of Associate Pastor By Worship Attendance

Church Attendance	0-99	100-299	300-499	500-749	750-999	1,000+
Number Of Respondents	3	82	95	95	56	80
Salary (100%*)	16,700	24,665	27,414	33,599	36,561	39,480
Annual % Increase (73%)	3%	5%	5%	5%	4%	5%
Parsonage (8%)	0	10,128	7,767	13,429	11,320	17,967
Housing (89%)	6,500	14,402	18,899	19,788	21,175	23,374
Housing (67%)	4,930	3,633	3,793	5,030	4,099	4,195
Life Insurance (38%)	0	565	652	1,179	908	1,105
Health Insurance (80%)	0	6,344	7,746	8,622	8,074	6,895
Vacation/weeks (93%)	3	3	3	3	4	4
Education Fund (45%)	0	1,119	1,192	1,408	1,494	1,717
Receive Auto Allow. (89%)	78%	82%	91%	91%	93%	93%

* The percentage following each compensation item indicates the portion of all associate pastors who received that form of compensation. The averages in each column are for those individuals who actually received that compensation item. See Chapter 3 for a full explanation of how to read this table.

Total Compensation Comparisons

Church Attendance	0-99	100-299	300-499	500-749	750-999	Over 1,000
Average attendance	78	201	373	595	851	2,575
Average church income	240,000	339,075	728,271	1,060,333	1,687,714	3,090,099
Average years employed	1	4	6	7	7	10
Annual compensation*	24,320	44,590	53,859	63,904	67,764	73,136
Standard deviation	14,956	15,616	15,379	18,191	14,327	20,858
Median compensation	12,000	41,300	53,226	62,700	68,215	70,398

National average for all associate pastors: $59,742 with a standard deviation of $19,943 (see Chapter 4, Table 4-3).

Total respondents: 411

* includes base salary, housing or parsonage allowance, retirement contribution, life and health insurance payments, and educational funds.

Table 6-2: Annual Compensation Of Associate Pastor By Church Income

Church Income in $	0-249,999	250,000-499,999	500,000-749,000	750,000-999,999	1,000,000 +
Number Of Respondents	34	66	62	51	178
Salary (100%*)	26,267	23,459	28,935	29,897	37,490
Annual % Increase (73%)	5%	6%	5%	4%	5%
Parsonage (8%)	6,570	9,545	9,917	15,150	16,178
Housing (89%)	14,054	15,506	16,854	19,049	22,570
Housing (67%)	4,044	3,573	3,916	4,318	4,515
Life Insurance (38%)	278	514	626	982	1,114
Health Insurance (80%)	6,549	6,802	7,459	8,581	7,742
Vacation/weeks (93%)	3	3	3	4	4
Education Fund (45%)	980	1,150	1,340	1,194	1,567
Receive Auto Allow. (89%)	74%	82%	87%	92%	94%

* The percentage following each compensation item indicates the portion of all associate pastors who received that form of compensation. The averages in each column are for those individuals who actually received that compensation item. See Chapter 3 for a full explanation of how to read this table.

Total Compensation Comparisons

Church Budget	0-249,999	250,000-499,999	500,000-749,999	750,000-999,999	Over 1,000,000
Average attendance	259	275	406	576	1,505
Average church income	188,215	365,145	605,895	866,484	2,212,628
Average years employed	5	4	6	7	8
Annual compensation*	41,707	46,205	53,832	60,063	70,493
Standard deviation	17,926	13,340	16,303	17,303	18,064
Median compensation	38,500	43,783	53,112	57,326	69,075

National average for all associate pastors: $59,742 with a standard deviation of $19,943 (see Chapter 4, Table 4-3)

Total respondents: 391

* includes base salary, housing or parsonage allowance, retirement contribution, life and health insurance payments, and educational funds.

Table 6-3: Annual Compensation Of Associate Pastor By Church Setting And Size

Attendance 0-250	Urban	Suburban	Medium City	Small Town	Rural
Number Of Respondents	13	26	19	21	8
Salary (100%*)	26,601	23,852	26,737	22,695	25,119
Annual % Increase (73%)	4%	5%	5%	6%	4%
Parsonage (8%)	1,200	19,987	1,000	4,750	0
Housing (89%)	17,277	18,399	14,281	11,065	9,726
Housing (67%)	5,894	4,187	4,300	4,370	2,582
Life Insurance (38%)	529	629	150	343	230
Health Insurance (80%)	8,787	7,259	7,694	4,849	6,286
Vacation/weeks (93%)	3	3	3	3	2
Education Fund (45%)	884	1,422	1,025	1,201	633
Receive Auto Allow. (89%)	92%	88%	68%	71%	62%

* The percentage following each compensation item indicates the portion of all associate pastors who received that form of compensation. The averages in each column are for those individuals who actually received that compensation item. See Chapter 3 for a full explanation of how to read this table.

Total Compensation Comparisons

Church Size: 0-250	Urban	Suburban	Medium City	Small Town	Rural
Average attendance	192	183	175	193	183
Average church income	364,375	414,903	405,059	271,577	331,824
Average years employed	3	4	4	5	1
Annual compensation*	55,469	49,985	43,857	36,937	39,790
Standard deviation	19,588	17,840	14,688	12,713	19,772
Median compensation	48,051	44,920	40,000	34,800	24,183

National average for all associate pastors: $59,742 with a standard deviation of $19,943 (see Chapter 4, Table 4-3)

Total respondents: 85

* includes base salary, housing or parsonage allowance, retirement contribution, life and health insurance payments, and educational funds.

Table 6-4: Annual Compensation Of Associate Pastor By Church Setting And Size

Attendance 251-500	Urban	Suburban	Medium City	Small Town	Rural
Number Of Respondents	13	51	24	29	7
Salary (100%*)	30,689	29,982	26,547	25,592	31,846
Annual % Increase (73%)	4%	5%	5%	4%	7%
Parsonage (8%)	9,800	9,500	1,000	13,000	0
Housing (89%)	18,795	19,391	16,599	17,654	15,644
Housing (67%)	6,155	3,541	4,091	3,218	3,862
Life Insurance (38%)	1,702	330	778	454	548
Health Insurance (80%)	6,449	7,361	8,896	7,464	6,001
Vacation/weeks (93%)	4	3	3	3	3
Education Fund (45%)	1,036	1,423	1,011	1,235	1,075
Receive Auto Allow. (89%)	100%	94%	88%	93%	86%

* The percentage following each compensation item indicates the portion of all associate pastors who received that form of compensation. The averages in each column are for those individuals who actually received that compensation item. See Chapter 3 for a full explanation of how to read this table.

Total Compensation Comparisons

Church Size: 251-500	Urban	Suburban	Medium City	Small Town	Rural
Average attendance	390	387	391	364	398
Average church income	1,127,928	700,941	740,680	599,054	416,781
Average years employed	5	7	9	5	6
Annual compensation*	56,431	57,073	51,035	52,187	54,833
Standard deviation	16,925	15,081	17,802	15,634	7,132
Median compensation	53,168	54,990	53,226	51,622	51,078

National average for all associate pastors: $59,742 with a standard deviation of $19,943 (see Chapter 4, Table 4-3)

Total respondents: 124

* includes base salary, housing or parsonage allowance, retirement contribution, life and health insurance payments, and educational funds.

Table 6-5: Annual Compensation Of Associate Pastor By Church Setting And Size

Attendance 501-750	Urban	Suburban	Medium City	Small Town	Rural
Number Of Respondents	13	34	22	15	2
Salary (100%*)	35,422	34,853	32,636	35,392	25,370
Annual % Increase (73%)	6%	4%	4%	6%	3%
Parsonage (8%)	0	22,650	0	5,600	12,000
Housing (89%)	22,045	21,224	20,408	19,547	12,000
Housing (67%)	7,962	5,016	4,253	5,352	2,800
Life Insurance (38%)	534	2,003	454	434	188
Health Insurance (80%)	11,174	9,032	8,801	8,073	7,110
Vacation/weeks (93%)	4	3	4	3	4
Education Fund (45%)	1,267	1,457	1,071	2,300	600
Receive Auto Allow. (89%)	92%	94%	86%	87%	100%

* The percentage following each compensation item indicates the portion of all associate pastors who received that form of compensation. The averages in each column are for those individuals who actually received that compensation item. See Chapter 3 for a full explanation of how to read this table.

Total Compensation Comparisons

Church Size: 0501-750	Urban	Suburban	Medium City	Small Town	Rural
Average attendance	649	639	635	621	530
Average church income	1,491,239	1,391,690	1,002,202	983,984	602,500
Average years employed	6	7	6	7	8
Annual compensation*	72,753	69,103	59,637	64,636	46,274
Standard deviation	13,299	18,857	17,873	16,994	19,976
Median compensation	71,110	71,506	60,459	62,700	

National average for all associate pastors: $59,742 with a standard deviation of $19,943 (see Chapter 4, Table 4-3)

Total respondents: 86

* includes base salary, housing or parsonage allowance, retirement contribution, life and health insurance payments, and educational funds.

Table 6-6: Annual Compensation Of Associate Pastor By Church Setting And Size

Attendance 751-1,000	Urban	Suburban	Medium City	Small Town	Rural
Number Of Respondents	5	27	14	5	0
Salary (100%*)	43,309	34,905	36,620	32,267	
Annual % Increase (73%)	3%	4%	5%	3%	
Parsonage (8%)	12,000	2,000	14,200	0	
Housing (89%)	17,013	23,267	20,327	17,774	
Housing (67%)	4,171	4,447	2,637	2,794	
Life Insurance (38%)	234	1,441	261	260	
Health Insurance (80%)	9,139	7,082	8,229	7,311	
Vacation/weeks (93%)	4	4	3	3	
Education Fund (45%)	625	1,542	1,900	1,125	
Receive Auto Allow. (89%)	80%	93%	93%	100%	

* The percentage following each compensation item indicates the portion of all associate pastors who received that form of compensation. The averages in each column are for those individuals who actually received that compensation item. See Chapter 3 for a full explanation of how to read this table.

Total Compensation Comparisons

Church Size: 751-1000	Urban	Suburban	Medium City	Small Town	Rural
Average attendance	907	883	909	826	
Average church income	2,129,254	1,600,203	1,649,578	1,531,097	
Average years employed	6	6	9	8	
Annual compensation*	73,666	67,614	67,486	55,632	
Standard deviation	21,474	14,733	13,989	9,805	
Median compensation	60,138	66,112	64,682	53,565	

National average for all associate pastors: $59,742 with a standard deviation of $19,943 (see Chapter 4, Table 4-3)

Total respondents: 51

* includes base salary, housing or parsonage allowance, retirement contribution, life and health insurance payments, and educational funds.

Table 6-7: Annual Compensation Of Associate Pastor By Church Setting And Size

Attendance Over 1,000	Urban	Suburban	Medium City	Small Town	Rural
Number Of Respondents	14	31	23	5	0
Salary (100%*)	43,578	39,436	40,028	36,251	
Annual % Increase (73%)	5%	4%	6%	3%	
Parsonage (8%)	0	25,000	16,560	0	
Housing (89%)	25,025	24,666	22,425	14,692	
Housing (67%)	5,216	4,427	3,655	3,341	
Life Insurance (38%)	221	903	2,276	141	
Health Insurance (80%)	6,929	7,182	6,230	6,921	
Vacation/weeks (93%)	4	4	4	2	
Education Fund (45%)	1,096	1,960	1,965	1,100	
Receive Auto Allow. (89%)	93%	94%	91%	80%	

* The percentage following each compensation item indicates the portion of all associate pastors who received that form of compensation. The averages in each column are for those individuals who actually received that compensation item. See Chapter 3 for a full explanation of how to read this table.

Total Compensation Comparisons

Church Size: 1,000 +	Urban	Suburban	Medium City	Small Town	Rural
Average attendance	4,287	2,683	2,121	1,262	
Average church income	4,521,069	3,553,197	2,156,559	2,001,538	
Average years employed	9	12	8	1	
Annual compensation*	75,536	74,389	74,609	60,842	
Standard deviation	32,413	19,335	15,812	14,165	
Median compensation	77,582	65,940	72,000	53,271	

National average for all associate pastors: $59,742 with a standard deviation of $19,943 (see Chapter 4, Table 4-3)

Total respondents: 45

* includes base salary, housing or parsonage allowance, retirement contribution, life and health insurance payments, and educational funds.

Table 6-8: Annual Compensation Of Associate Pastor By Gender

Gender	Male	Female
Number Of Respondents	381	46
Salary (100%*)	31,918	29,924
Annual % Increase (73%)	5%	4%
Parsonage (8%)	11,900	11,867
Housing (89%)	19,774	16,768
Housing (67%)	4,065	6,015
Life Insurance (38%)	878	1,189
Health Insurance (80%)	7,581	7,483
Vacation/weeks (93%)	3	4
Education Fund (45%)	1,402	1,197
Receive Auto Allow. (89%)	90%	83%

* The percentage following each compensation item indicates the portion of all associate pastors who received that form of compensation. The averages in each column are for those individuals who actually received that compensation item. See Chapter 3 for a full explanation of how to read this table.

Total Compensation Comparisons

Gender	Male	Female
Average attendance	898	738
Average church income	1,319,236	1,063,484
Average years employed	7	5
Annual compensation*	60,221	55,779
Standard deviation	19,886	20,194
Median compensation	60,459	53,477

National average for all associate pastors: $59,742 with a standard deviation of $19,943 (see Chapter 4, Table 4-3)

Total respondents: 427

* includes base salary, housing or parsonage allowance, retirement contribution, life and health insurance payments, and educational funds.

Table 6-9: Annual Compensation Of Associate Pastor By Education

Highest Degree	High School	Associate	Bachelor	Master	Doctorate
Number Of Respondents	17	5	101	201	39
Salary (100%*)	25,242	22,750	27,924	33,311	39,245
Annual % Increase (73%)	7%	3%	5%	5%	4%
Parsonage (8%)	0	20,000	9,379	13,098	11,733
Housing (89%)	22,916	20,067	18,404	19,477	20,568
Housing (67%)	2,437	3,700	3,658	4,602	4,854
Life Insurance (38%)	410	326	755	740	1,065
Health Insurance (80%)	8,375	7,009	7,209	8,189	6,401
Vacation/weeks (93%)	3	3	3	3	4
Education Fund (45%)	914	0	1,363	1,367	1,146
Receive Auto Allow. (89%)	94%	80%	85%	93%	85%

* The percentage following each compensation item indicates the portion of all associate pastors who received that form of compensation. The averages in each column are for those individuals who actually received that compensation item. See Chapter 3 for a full explanation of how to read this table.

Total Compensation Comparisons

Highest Degree	High School	Associate	Bachelor	Masters	Doctorate
Average attendance	750	475	963	866	995
Average church income	1,215,220	724,000	1,056,533	1,283,990	1,962,940
Average years employed	8	11	6	6	9
Annual compensation*	52,473	45,411	53,313	63,075	68,379
Standard deviation	16,557	28,965	20,606	17,201	23,507
Median compensation	48,000	44,700	53,271	62,700	61,313

National average for all associate pastors: $59,742 with a standard deviation of $19,943 (see Chapter 4, Table 4-3)

Total respondents: 363

* includes base salary, housing or parsonage allowance, retirement contribution, life and health insurance payments, and educational funds.

Table 6-10: Annual Compensation Of Associate Pastor By Years Employed

Years Employed	0-5	6-10	11-15	over 15
Number Of Respondents	231	110	38	36
Salary (100%*)	29,642	34,179	31,964	38,565
Annual % Increase (73%)	5%	5%	5%	4%
Parsonage (8%)	11,377	13,243	12,200	15,667
Housing (89%)	18,159	21,230	19,171	22,461
Housing (67%)	4,366	4,072	3,605	4,694
Life Insurance (38%)	688	1,759	706	2445
Health Insurance (80%)	7,466	7,744	7,534	7,944
Vacation/weeks (93%)	3	3	4	4
Education Fund (45%)	1,365	1,406	1,605	1,290
Receive Auto Allow. (89%)	87%	92%	89%	94%

* The percentage following each compensation item indicates the portion of all associate pastors who received that form of compensation. The averages in each column are for those individuals who actually received that compensation item. See Chapter 3 for a full explanation of how to read this table.

Total Compensation Comparisons

Years Employed	0-5	6-10	11-15	Over 15
Average attendance	735	1,131	943	1,049
Average church income	1,117,379	1,342,571	1,415,987	2,199,033
Average years employed	3	8	13	22
Annual compensation*	56,074	62,972	62,647	72,608
Standard deviation	18,673	20,910	14,559	22,405
Median compensation	56,802	62,400	65,027	74,712

National average for all associate pastors: $59,742 with a standard deviation of $19,943 (see Chapter 4, Table 4-3)

Total respondents: 415

* includes base salary, housing or parsonage allowance, retirement contribution, life and health insurance payments, and educational funds.

Table 6-11: Annual Compensation Of Part-Time Associate Pastors By Hours Worked

Hours Per Week	1-14	15-29	30-39	All Part-time
Number of Respondents	8	15	7	59**
Salary (95%*)	7,379	8,785	19,101	10,883
Annual % Increase (53%)	2%	5%	3%	4%
Parsonage (2%)	0	19,350	0	19,350
Housing (44%)	4,622	12,736	19,335	12,591
Retirement (22%)	957	1,170	3,467	1,871
Life Insurance (10%)	0	444	100	234
Health Insurance (31%)	4,514	2,787	4,440	4,381
Vacation/weeks (53%)	3	3	3	3
Education Funds (20%)	0	450	450	583
Receive Auto Allow. (73%)	100%	93%	86%	73%

* The percentage following each compensation item indicates the portion of all part-time associate pastors who received that form of compensation. The averages in each column are for those individuals who actually received that compensation item. See Chapter 3 for a full explanation of how to read this table.

Total Compensation Comparisons

Hours Worked Per Week	1-14	15-29	30-39	All Part-time
Average attendance	395	334	555	370
Average church income	270,077	548,131	1,038,230	564,686
Average years employed	3	8	4	5
Average hours per week	10	21	31	20
Average compensation	10,135	17,231	42,602	18,410
Ave. hourly compensation*	19.49	15.78	26.43	17.70
Ave. hourly salary**	14.19	8.04	11.85	10.46

* includes base salary, housing or parsonage allowance, retirement contribution, life and health insurance payments, and educational funds.

** includes base salary only; see discussion on "rounding errors" in Chapter 3.

Chapter 7

Christian Education Directors

Employment Profile

A majority of the Christian Education Directors participating in this study serve as ordained ministers. The vast majority are college graduates, and 43% have graduate degrees. Christian Education Directors reflected the following profile:

	Full-time	Part-time
☐ Number of Respondents	243	98
☐ Ordained	55%	12%
☐ Average Years Employed	6	4
☐ Male	55%	13%
☐ Female	45%	87%
☐ Self-employed	1%	2%
☐ Church Employee	99%	98%
☐ High School Diploma	9%	16%
☐ Associate Degree	4%	9%
☐ Bachelor Degree	44%	56%
☐ Master Degree	38%	16%
☐ Doctorate	5%	3%

Compensation Analysis

The analysis below is based upon the tables found later in this chapter. The tables present compensation data according to worship attendance, church income, combinations of size and setting, gender, education, and years employed for CE Directors who serve full-time. The final table provides data for part-time CE directors based upon the number of hours worked. In this way, the CE Director's compensation can be viewed from a variety of useful perspectives. The total compensation amount found in a separate box at the bottom of each page includes the base salary, housing or parsonage amount, life and health insurance payments, retirement contribution, and educational funds.

Key Points

✎ *CE Directors are closely aligned with youth ministers in compensation trends, although, generally, the earnings of CE Directors increase more rapidly in large congregations.* Most full-time CE Directors serve in churches with an attendance over 500, with about one-third in congregations over 1,000. Overall compensation remains below the national average until a position is secured in a larger church with an average attendance over 600. *See Table 7-1.*

✎ *Both church income and size correlate with compensation.* Compensation increased directly with the size of the church budget. From the standpoint of compensation, CE Directors are aligned with youth ministers and church administrators, but generally have higher levels of compensation in larger churches than youth ministers. Income increases significantly once the church budget exceeds $1,000,000 per year. *See Table 7-2.*

✎ *CE Directors who work in churches with an average attendance under 500 have an annual compensation below the national average regardless of church setting.* Most CE Directors work in larger suburban churches, while very few work in rural settings. Overall compensation was higher in medium size cities, suburban and urban churches. *See Tables 7-3 and 7-4.*

✎ *Significant gender differences exists for CE Directors.* Women earned 69% of the compensation of their male counterparts. A disparity of over $15,000 - $20,000 in annual total compensation has existed the past several years. Women worked in smaller churches with an average attendance significantly less than men. In addition, overall church income was $800,000 less in those churches with female CE Directors, yet in both cases, average church income exceeded $1,000,000. Women in this study were also less likely to receive fringe benefits. The difference in overall compensation can be attributed to gender more than any other variable. *See Table 7-5.*

✎ *Educational achievement had a relationship to compensation.* Overall compensation increased steadily with education. Yet, even college graduates were still below the national average. Fourty-five percent of the full-time Christian education directors surveyed had either a master's degree or a doctorate. Those with doctoral degrees earned on average nearly $19,000 more than the typical CE DIrector. *See Table 7-6.*

✎ *Employment longevity impacted overall compensation.* Compensation increased some-what with years of service. Those CE Directors with the most years of service tended to work in congregations with the largest incomes. Those with five or less years of service were below the national average. *See Table 7-7.*

✎ *Many CE Directors work part-time.* Hourly compensation varied with the number of hours worked. Those who work more hours take more of their compensation as fringe benefits. The typical part-time CE Director worked 20 hours per week, and had been in the church for about four years. Fairly high turnover exists. *See Table 7-8.*

Benefit Analysis

Full-time staff members. Full-time Christian education directors received benefit packages comparable to those of other professional and ministerial staff members within the church. Yet, since fewer are ordained, a smaller percentage received parsonage and housing allowances compared to ministerial staff members. In general, the Christian education director's average benefits are slightly less than those of associate pastors.

Part-time staff members. Nearly 90% of part-time Christian education directors are female. Ninety-nine percent of part-time directors are church employees. Many part-time Christian education directors serve congregations with an attendance between 250-500. Part-time Christian education directors received few benefits with the most common being an auto allowance and a two week paid vacation.

Benefits	Full-time	Part-time
☐ Housing allowance	51%	9%
☐ Parsonage provided	4%	0%
☐ Retirement	58%	10%
☐ Life insurance	39%	7%
☐ Health insurance	76%	12%
☐ Paid vacation	96%	55%
☐ Auto allowance	88%	74%
☐ Continuing education funds	41%	31%

Eleven Year Compensation Trend: National Averages for Christian Education Directors

☐	1993	$35,291
☐	1994	$37,676
☐	1995	$37,453
☐	1996	$38,855
☐	1997	$40,863
☐	1998	$41,428
☐	1999	$45,620
☐	2000	$47,331
☐	2001	$48,440
☐	2002	$49,351
☐	2003	$50,313

Table 7-1: Annual Compensation Of CE Director By Worship Attendance

Church Attendance	0-99	100-299	300-499	500-749	750-999	over 1000
Number Of Respondents	0	23	47	48	46	74
Salary (100%*)		27,326	30,949	30,870	34,563	34,573
Annual % Increase (71%)		4%	4%	4%	4%	4%
Parsonage (4%)		1,020	7,100	13,974	8,750	21,800
Housing (51%)		8,671	18,336	19,717	20,122	20,720
Retirement (58%)		2,953	3,022	3,026	3,396	3,856
Life Insurance (39%)		523	609	278	602	462
Health Insurance (76%)		4,220	6,217	6,221	7,414	6,700
Vacation/weeks (96%)		3	3	3	3	3
Education Fund (41%)		562	1,037	1,241	1,500	1,364
Auto Allowance (88%)		74%	91%	85%	91%	93%

* The percentage following each compensation item indicates the portion of CE Directors who received that form of compensation. The averages in each column are for those individuals who actually received that compensation item. See Chapter 3 for a full explanation of how to read this table.

Total Compensation Comparisons

Church Attendance	0-99	100-299	300-499	500-749	750-999	Over 1,000
Average attendance		178	388	604	854	2,734
Average church income		368,973	875,441	1,174,386	1,742,363	3,128,394
Average years employed		6	6	5	5	7
Average compensation*		32,799	43,805	48,317	54,177	59,753
Standard deviation		7,511	13,867	16,140	14,466	17,935
Median compensation		30,569	42,791	47,578	52,529	57,484

National average for all CE Directors: $50,313 with a standard deviation of $17,403 (see Chapter 4, Table 4-3).

Total respondents: 238

* includes base salary, housing or parsonage allowance, retirement contribution, life and health insurance payments, and educational funds.

Table 7-2: Annual Compensation Of CE Director By Church Budget

Church Budget in $	0-249,999	250,000-499,999	500,000-749,000	750,000-999,999	1,000,000 +
Number Of Respondents	11	15	22	30	141
Salary (100%*)	28,253	27,743	30,869	29,163	34,278
Annual % Increase (71%)	3%	3%	4%	3%	4%
Parsonage (4%)	1,020	0	5,200	15,500	13,410
Housing (51%)	2,685	15,000	15,617	15,530	21,098
Retirement (58%)	3,182	2,079	2,913	2,615	3,704
Life Insurance (39%)	639	760	334	214	556
Health Insurance (76%)	2,872	4,545	5,330	6,261	6,742
Vacation/weeks (96%)	3	3	3	3	3
Education Fund (41%)	500	643	1,214	1,339	1,292
Auto Allowance (88%)	73%	67%	82%	83%	93%

* The percentage following each compensation item indicates the portion of CE Directors who received that form of compensation. The averages in each column are for those individuals who actually received that compensation item. See Chapter 3 for a full explanation of how to read this table.

Total Compensation Comparisons

Church Budget	0-249,999	250,000-499,999	500,000-749,999	750,000-999,999	1,000,000+
Average attendance	343	271	412	651	1,715
Average church income	170,741	336,043	650,202	864,348	2,392,873
Average years employed	5	4	7	6	6
Average compensation*	32,141	32,933	40,845	44,683	56,699
Standard deviation	10,467	9,483	11,674	16,158	16,298
Median compensation	26,085	32,449	41,273	42,612	54,235

National average for all CE Directors: $50,313 with a standard deviation of $17,403 (see Chapter 4, Table 4-3).

Total respondents: 219

* includes base salary, housing or parsonage allowance, retirement contribution, life and health insurance payments, and educational funds.

Table 7-3: Annual Compensation Of CE Director By Church Setting And Size

Attendance Under 500	Urban	Suburban	Medium City	Small Town	Rural
Number Of Respondents	14	25	16	17	0
Salary (100%*)	31,796	31,287	26,448	29,151	
Annual % Increase (71%)	3%	5%	3%	3%	
Parsonage (4%)	0	0	5,200	5,010	
Housing (51%)	29,000	17,522	17,765	8,346	
Retirement (58%)	3,675	2,598	2,875	3,110	
Life Insurance (39%)	1,424	282	245	43	
Health Insurance (76%)	5,566	6,870	4,716	4,585	
Vacation/weeks (96%)	3	3	3	3	
Education Fund (41%)	1,050	846	658	914	
Auto Allowance (88%)	93%	92%	69%	82%	

* The percentage following each compensation item indicates the portion of CE Directors who received that form of compensation. The averages in each column are for those individuals who actually received that compensation item. See Chapter 3 for a full explanation of how to read this table.

Total Compensation Comparisons

Church Size: Under 500	Urban	Suburban	Medium City	Small Town	Rural
Average attendance	326	336	280	297	
Average church income	925,258	775,193	575,023	567,780	
Average years employed	6	8	4	6	
Average compensation*	40,965	43,686	36,184	37,634	
Standard deviation	13,136	11,589	14,965	12,100	
Median compensation	36,928	41,101	33,575	32,800	

National average for all CE Directors: $50,313 with a standard deviation of $17,403 (see Chapter 4, Table 4-3).

Total respondents: 72

* includes base salary, housing or parsonage allowance, retirement contribution, life and health insurance payments, and educational funds.

Table 7-4: Annual Compensation Of CE Director By Church Setting And Size

Attendance Over 499	Urban	Suburban	Medium City	Small Town	Rural
Number Of Respondents	24	75	43	20	4
Salary (100%*)	37,429	34,619	30,725	32,464	28,233
Annual % Increase (71%)	4%	4%	4%	4%	6%
Parsonage (4%)	0	17,316	12,367	0	0
Housing (51%)	22,821	21,242	18,612	19,698	14,400
Retirement (58%)	3,488	4,086	2,676	3,502	2,754
Life Insurance (39%)	393	638	208	559	0
Health Insurance (76%)	5,976	6,990	7,394	5,375	7,842
Vacation/weeks (96%)	3	3	3	3	3
Education Fund (41%)	1,615	1,300	1,493	900	1,000
Auto Allowance (88%)	96%	89%	91%	85%	100%

* The percentage following each compensation item indicates the portion of CE Directors who received that form of compensation. The averages in each column are for those individuals who actually received that compensation item. See Chapter 3 for a full explanation of how to read this table.

Total Compensation Comparisons

Attendance Over 499	Urban	Suburban	Medium City	Small Town	Rural
Average attendance	2,634	1,639	1,461	841	955
Average church income	3,226,195	2,388,240	1,749,011	1,357,367	1,253,750
Average years employed	7	5	7	6	6
Average compensation*	62,259	54,934	55,178	51,052	42,253
Standard deviation	19,919	16,474	14,783	18,559	11,263
Median compensation	59,610	51,900	51,515	52,529	39,076

National average for all CE Directors: $50,313 with a standard deviation of $17,403 (see Chapter 4, Table 4-3).

Total respondents: 166

* includes base salary, housing or parsonage allowance, retirement contribution, life and health insurance payments, and educational funds.

Table 7-5: Annual Compensation Of CE Director By Gender

Gender	Male	Female
Number Of Respondents	134	109
Salary (100%*)	33,348	30,926
Annual % Increase (71%)	4%	4%
Parsonage (4%)	12,341	10,073
Housing (51%)	20,115	18,148
Retirement (58%)	3,466	3,291
Life Insurance (39%)	388	671
Health Insurance (76%)	7,141	5,279
Vacation/weeks (96%)	3	3
Education Fund (41%)	1,404	914
Auto Allowance (88%)	90%	86%

* The percentage following each compensation item indicates the portion of CE Directors who received that form of compensation. The averages in each column are for those individuals who actually received that compensation item. See Chapter 3 for a full explanation of how to read this table.

Total Compensation Comparisons

Gender	Male	Female
Average attendance	1,525	845
Average church income	2,116,673	1,310,523
Average years employed	7	6
Average compensation*	58,384	40,392
Standard deviation	16,240	13,179
Median compensation	58,349	39,295

National average for all CE Directors: $50,313 with a standard deviation of $17,403 (see Chapter 4, Table 4-3).

Total respondents: 243

* includes base salary, housing or parsonage allowance, retirement contribution, life and health insurance payments, and educational funds.

Table 7-6: Annual Compensation Of CE Director By Education

Highest Degree	High School	Associate	Bachelor	Master	Doctorate
Number Of Respondents	18	9	91	78	11
Salary (100%*)	26,817	33,036	28,940	36,995	34,866
Annual % Increase (71%)	4%	3%	3%	5%	4%
Parsonage (4%)	5,200	0	20,333	7,614	0
Housing (51%)	18,575	15,300	19,157	18,708	25,916
Retirement (58%)	2,432	1,977	3,306	3,799	3,685
Life Insurance (39%)	169	149	714	346	488
Health Insurance (76%)	4,791	7,028	6,152	6,821	7,434
Vacation/weeks (96%)	3	3	3	3	4
Education Fund (41%)	736	0	1,076	1,310	1,614
Auto Allowance (88%)	83%	100%	87%	95%	91%

* The percentage following each compensation item indicates the portion of CE Directors who received that form of compensation. The averages in each column are for those individuals who actually received that compensation item. See Chapter 3 for a full explanation of how to read this table.

Total Compensation Comparisons

Highest Degree	High School	Associate	Bachelor	Master	Doctorate
Average attendance	1,855	680	1,410	1,067	1,256
Average church income	1,157,892	1,259,009	1,552,023	2,212,233	2,287,089
Average years employed	7	8	5	7	7
Average compensation*	38,054	41,016	44,968	58,656	69,344
Standard deviation	14,825	10,909	15,420	17,001	16,627
Median compensation	34,699	34,299	42,791	61,000	63,600

National average for all CE Directors: $50,313 with a standard deviation of $17,403 (see Chapter 4, Table 4-3).

Total respondents: 207

* includes base salary, housing or parsonage allowance, retirement contribution, life and health insurance payments, and educational funds.

Table 7-7: Annual Compensation Of CE Director By Years Employed

Years Employed	0-5	6-10	11-15	over 15
Number Of Respondents	142	53	29	14
Salary (100%*)	30,176	34,698	33,633	40,882
Annual % Increase (71%)	4%	4%	4%	3%
Parsonage (4%)	13,595	10,100	0	2,500
Housing (51%)	19,611	19,196	21,208	20,313
Retirement (58%)	3,325	3,221	3,364	4,107
Life Insurance (39%)	494	554	503	254
Health Insurance (76%)	6,042	7,017	6,626	7,332
Vacation/weeks (96%)	3	3	4	4
Education Fund (41%)	1,131	1,318	928	1,546
Auto Allowance (88%)	85%	94%	90%	93%

* The percentage following each compensation item indicates the portion of CE Directors who received that form of compensation. The averages in each column are for those individuals who actually received that compensation item. See Chapter 3 for a full explanation of how to read this table.

Total Compensation Comparisons

Years Employed	0-5	6-10	11-15	Over 15
Average attendance	1,180	1,435	1,145	1,171
Average church income	1,711,207	1,904,551	1,441,040	2,334,546
Average years employed	3	8	13	20
Average compensation*	46,931	54,150	53,589	61,535
Standard deviation	15,851	19,381	16,859	18,884
Median compensation	45,000	53,471	52,679	55,121

National average for all CE Directors: $50,313 with a standard deviation of $17,403 (see Chapter 4, Table 4-3).

Total respondents: 238

* includes base salary, housing or parsonage allowance, retirement contribution, life and health insurance payments, and educational funds.

Table 7-8: Annual Compensation Of Part-Time CE Directors By Hours Worked

Hours-per-week	1-14	15-29	30-39	All Part-time
Number Of Respondents	9	35	8	98
Salary (100%*)	14,538	14,616	23,071	14,818
Annual % Increase (59%)	5%	4%	7%	5%
Parsonage (0%)	0	0	0	0
Housing (9%)	5,385	13,510	16,884	12,245
Retirement (10%)	0	1,750	1,219	1,976
Life Insurance (7%)	0	100	339	215
Health Insurance (12%)	0	3,945	3,252	5,963
Vacation/weeks (55%)	1	2	3	2
Education Funds (31%)	0	704	975	657
Auto Allowance (74%)	89%	89%	88%	74%

* The percentage following each compensation item indicates the portion of part-time CE Directors who received that form of compensation. The averages in each column are for those individuals who actually received that compensation item. See Chapter 3 for a full explanation of how to read this table.

Total Compensation Comparisons

Hours Worked Per Week	1-14	15-29	30 -39	All Part-time
Average attendance	363	509	774	444
Average church income	590,472	852,982	965,276	693,965
Average years employed	6	4	7	4
Average hours per week	9	21	31	20
Average compensation	15,136	16,770	26,617	17,091
Ave. hourly compensation*	32.34	15.36	16.51	16.43
Average hourly salary**	31.06	13.38	14.31	14.25

Total respondents: 98

* includes base salary, housing or parsonage allowance, retirement contribution, life and health insurance payments, and educational funds (note: auto allowance is included in base salary).

** includes base salary only; see discussion on ''rounding errors'' in Chapter 3.

Chapter 8

Youth Ministers

Employment Profile

On average, youth ministers are employed for a shorter period than other staff members. Few congregations under 100 in attendance have a youth minister. However, a church is more likely to have a youth minister than an associate pastor, Christian Education Director, choir director, business administrator, bookkeeper, or custodian. After pastors, only church secretaries serve on church staffs more frequently than youth ministers. The typical youth minister is ordained, has a college degree, and is a male. The youth ministers surveyed provided the following statistical profile:

	Full-time	Part-time
☐ Number of Respondents	479	91
☐ Ordained	68%	20%
☐ Average Years Employed	4	3
☐ Male	91%	70%
☐ Female	9%	30%
☐ Self-employed	1%	3%
☐ Church Employee	99%	97%
☐ High School Diploma	8%	22%
☐ Associate Degree	2%	2%
☐ Bachelor Degree	60%	60%
☐ Master Degree	28%	16%
☐ Doctorate	2%	0%

Compensation Analysis

The analysis below is based upon the tables found later in this chapter. The tables present compensation data according to worship attendance, church income, combinations of size and setting, gender, education, and years employed for youth pastors who serve full-time. The final table provides data for part-time youth pastors based upon the number of hours worked. In this way, the youth pastor's compensation can be viewed from a variety of useful perspectives. The total compensation amount found in a separate box at the bottom of each page includes the base salary, housing or parsonage amount, life and health insurance payments, retirement contribution, and educational funds.

Key Points

✎ *Church attendance directly impacted the compensation of youth ministers.* Those serving in congregations with an attendance less than 500 are below the national average; those in congregations above 500 are equal to or above the national average. Over one-half of youth ministers serve in the larger churches. *See Table 8-1.*

✎ *Church income impacts total compensation.* Neither church income nor church size, however, is decisive. Compensation levels increase more slowly for youth pastors than for other professional staff positions. The turnover rate for youth ministers is high, regardless of church size or budget. *See Table 8-2.*

✎ *Urban churches provided the best compensation for smaller congregations.* These congregations provided considerably more compensation than did churches in the other geographical categories with an attendance under 500, except for suburban churches. Yet all youth pastors in churches with an average attendance below 500 were below the national compensation average. *See Table 8-3.*

✎ *Geographical setting had an impact on compensation levels within larger congregations, although that varies from year to year.* Youth pastors in larger churches earned more than the national average. This was true regardless of geographical setting, except for rural areas. Those in urban churches earned the most this year, but that varies from one year to the next. *See Table 8-4.*

✎ *On average, women received higher salaries than men, although their total compensation was significantly lower.* Female youth pastors earned 75% of their male counterparts, down from 82% last year. Male youth ministers significantly outnumber female youth ministers. Both groups tended to serve in larger congregations with higher levels of income, but females were paid less than their male counterparts. The disparity in overall earnings is based on gender. *See Table 8-5.*

✎ *Educational achievement had a direct impact upon compensation levels of youth ministers, especially for those with a graduate degree.* Eighty-nine percent of the youth ministers had a bachelor's degree or higher. Yet, average compensation for those with a bachelor's degree was still below the national average. Having a graduate degree resulted in significant increases in compensation. *See Table 8-6.*

✎ *Over 90% of youth pastors served for less than ten years with 75% serving less than five years.* No clear variables exist that differentiate those who serve long periods from those who do not, although this year tenure increased with church income. Those with the longest tenure did receive the highest levels of compensation. *See Table 8-7.*

✎ *In general, part-time youth ministers receive among the lowest compensation of part-time professional staff members.* Most serve in congregations with an attendance below 350 people. *See Table 8-8.*

Benefits Analysis

Full-time staff members. Full-time youth ministers received benefits similar to other professional staff members. Youth ministers, though, were more likely to receive a housing allowance than those involved in education, music, or church administration.

Part-time staff members. Approximately 16% of the youth ministers in this sample worked part-time. Of this group, 30% were female compared to 9% for full-time youth ministers. Part-time workers often serve in smaller churches. Proportionately, salary for part-time workers was lower compared to those working full-time. Part-time workers also received only a small fraction of the benefits of full-time staff.

Benefits	Full-time	Part-time
☐ Housing allowance	66%	11%
☐ Parsonage provided	9%	2%
☐ Retirement	55%	9%
☐ Life insurance	35%	0%
☐ Health insurance	77%	5%
☐ Paid vacation	95%	47%
☐ Auto allowance	89%	66%
☐ Continuing education funds	41%	20%

Eleven Year Compensation Trend: National Averages for Youth Ministers

☐ 1993	$33,768
☐ 1994	$34,238
☐ 1995	$35,181
☐ 1996	$35,398
☐ 1997	$36,968
☐ 1998	$37,918
☐ 1999	$39,691
☐ 2000	$42,561
☐ 2001	$43,288
☐ 2002	$45,043
☐ 2003	$47,058

Table 8-1: Annual Compensation Of Youth Minister By Worship Attendance

Church Attendance	0-99	100-299	300-499	500-749	750-999	over 1000
Number Of Respondents	2	95	106	108	66	90
Salary (100%*)	18,500	24,715	26,361	27,743	28,928	31,146
Annual % Increase (71%)	0	6%	5%	5%	4%	5%
Parsonage (9%)	0	9,163	11,900	9,567	10,450	15,400
Housing (66%)	0	11,920	15,954	17,234	19,307	20,261
Retirement (55%)	0	2,545	2,238	3,051	3,237	3,018
Life Insurance (35%)	0	709	494	457	271	415
Health Insurance (77%)	1,000	5,632	5,989	7,069	6,280	6,579
Vacation/weeks (95%)	0	2	3	3	3	3
Education Funds (41%)	0	954	1,090	1,532	1,413	1,445
Auto Allowance (89%)	100%	81%	92%	91%	91%	92%

* The percentage following each compensation item indicates the portion of church administrators who received that form of compensation. The averages in each column are for those individuals who actually received that compensation item. See Chapter 3 for a full explanation of how to read this table.

Total Compensation Comparisons

Church Attendance	0-99	100-299	300-499	500-749	750-999	Over 1,000
Average attendance	85	206	383	600	854	2,431
Average church income	106,525	369,075	756,152	1,111,536	1,703,789	2,991,582
Average years employed	1	3	4	4	4	6
Average compensation*	19,000	37,052	45,660	48,147	49,528	56,940
Standard deviation	7,071	9,865	9,429	14,575	13,068	16,620
Median compensation		35,760	46,473	48,048	47,696	54,863

National Average for all Youth Ministers: $47,058 with a standard deviation of $14,492 (see Chapter 4, Table 4-3).

Total respondents: 476

* includes base salary, housing or parsonage allowance, retirement contribution, life and health insurance payments, and educational funds.

Table 8-2: Annual Compensation Of Youth Minister By Church Budget

Church Budget in $	0-249,999	250,000-499,999	500,000-749,000	750,000-999,999	1,000,000 +
Number Of Respondents	29	82	67	61	208
Salary (100%*)	23,251	23,533	27,128	26,365	30,217
Annual % Increase (71%)	5%	6%	6%	5%	5%
Parsonage (9%)	7,140	8,058	12,563	12,265	13,262
Housing (66%)	11,623	12,977	15,927	15,402	20,054
Retirement (55%)	4,178	1,700	2,547	2,666	3,136
Life Insurance (35%)	1,444	237	281	257	463
Health Insurance (77%)	5,296	5,325	6,996	5,849	6,763
Vacation/weeks (95%)	2	2	3	3	3
Education Funds (41%)	620	987	1,190	1,148	1,502
Auto Allowance (89%)	83%	80%	88%	89%	93%

* The percentage following each compensation item indicates the portion of church administrators who received that form of compensation. The averages in each column are for those individuals who actually received that compensation item. See Chapter 3 for a full explanation of how to read this table.

Total Compensation Comparisons

Church Budget	0-249,999	250,000-499,999	500,000-749,999	750,000-999,999	1,000,000+
Average attendance	278	262	413	582	1,407
Average church income	169,880	358,388	621,371	868,826	2,178,914
Average years employed	3	3	4	4	5
Average compensation*	35,223	37,605	45,861	43,581	53,866
Standard deviation	11,129	9,229	13,347	10,723	14,786
Median compensation	35,161	35,772	44,700	43,500	51,233

National Average for all Youth Ministers: $47,058 with a standard deviation of $14,492 (see Chapter 4, Table 4-3).

Total respondents: 447

* includes base salary, housing or parsonage allowance, retirement contribution, life and health insurance payments, and educational funds.

Table 8-3: Annual Compensation Of Youth Minister By Church Setting And Size

Attendance Under 500	Urban	Suburban	Medium City	Small Town	Rural
Number Of Respondents	15	79	43	51	11
Salary (100%*)	28,623	24,817	24,310	26,934	25,075
Annual % Increase (71%)	3%	6%	7%	5%	5%
Parsonage (9%)	0	12,622	7,050	9,744	10,260
Housing (.66%)	17,022	15,651	12,218	14,216	9,188
Retirement (55%)	3,171	2,382	2,408	2,236	1,713
Life Insurance (35%)	1,597	299	1,531	286	274
Health Insurance (77%)	5,595	6,520	4,523	6,236	4,714
Vacation/weeks (95%)	3	3	2	2	3
Education Funds (41%)	950	1,152	1,019	865	938
Auto Allowance (89%)	100%	91%	84%	84%	73%

* The percentage following each compensation item indicates the portion of church administrators who received that form of compensation. The averages in each column are for those individuals who actually received that compensation item. See Chapter 3 for a full explanation of how to read this table.

Total Compensation Comparisons

Church Size: Under 500	Urban	Suburban	Medium City	Small Town	Rural
Average attendance	351	302	267	308	241
Average church income	939,846	590,482	474,350	524,103	397,551
Average years employed	3	3	3	4	3
Average compensation*	44,907	43,118	36,216	42,767	37,480
Standard deviation	11,132	10,009	9,824	11,797	7,935
Median compensation	43,400	43,096	35,161	40,896	35,520

National Average for all Youth Ministers: $47,058 with a standard deviation of $14,492 (see Chapter 4, Table 4-3).

Total respondents: 199

* includes base salary, housing or parsonage allowance, retirement contribution, life and health insurance payments, and educational funds.

Table 8-4: Annual Compensation Of Youth Minister By Church Setting And Size

Attendance Over 499	Urban	Suburban	Medium City	Small Town	Rural
Number Of Respondents	31	113	76	35	8
Salary (100%*)	33,199	29,689	27,517	27,947	28,969
Annual % Increase (71%)	6%	4%	4%	7%	5%
Parsonage (9%)	0	13,157	13,817	8,000	0
Housing (66%)	23,817	20,479	17,257	14,916	12,734
Retirement (55%)	3,238	3,386	2,637	3,020	2,617
Life Insurance (35%)	243	562	175	533	129
Health Insurance (77%)	6,186	7,071	6,645	6,186	7,128
Vacation/weeks (95%)	3	3	3	3	3
Education Funds (41%)	1,438	1,482	1,387	1,779	1,000
Auto Allowance (89%)	90%	91%	91%	91%	100%

* The percentage following each compensation item indicates the portion of church administrators who received that form of compensation. The averages in each column are for those individuals who actually received that compensation item. See Chapter 3 for a full explanation of how to read this table.

Total Compensation Comparisons

Attendance Over 499	Urban	Suburban	Medium City	Small Town	Rural
Average attendance	2,216	1,302	1,175	787	859
Average church income	2,773,262	2,100,366	1,521,184	1,369,513	1,349,194
Average years employed	5	5	4	4	5
Average compensation*	56,406	53,849	48,616	47,469	46,161
Standard deviation	20,244	15,923	14,015	11,677	6,370
Median compensation	51,178	51,300	49,982	48,920	48,559

National Average for all Youth Ministers: $47,058 with a standard deviation of $14,492 (see Chapter 4, Table 4-3).

Total respondents: 263

* includes base salary, housing or parsonage allowance, retirement contribution, life and health insurance payments, and educational funds.

Table 8-5: Annual Compensation Of Youth Minister By Gender

Gender	Male	Female
Number Of Respondents	437	41
Salary (100%*)	27,572	28,524
Annual % Increase (71%)	5%	3%
Parsonage (9%)	11,088	8,400
Housing (66%)	17,191	11,713
Retirement (55%)	2,850	2,572
Life Insurance (35%)	456	352
Health Insurance (77%)	6,501	4,821
Vacation/weeks (95%)	3	3
Education Funds (41%)	1,361	788
Auto Allowance (89%)	89%	88%

* The percentage following each compensation item indicates the portion of church administrators who received that form of compensation. The averages in each column are for those individuals who actually received that compensation item. See Chapter 3 for a full explanation of how to read this table.

Total Compensation Comparisons

Gender	Male	Female
Average attendance	867	743
Average church income	1,330,501	981,192
Average years employed	4	4
Average compensation*	48,109	36,089
Standard deviation	14,427	10,162
Median compensation	47,227	35,000

National Average for all Youth Ministers: $47,058 with a standard deviation of $14,492 (see Chapter 4, Table 4-3).

Total respondents: 478

* includes base salary, housing or parsonage allowance, retirement contribution, life and health insurance payments, and educational funds.

Table 8-6: Annual Compensation Of Youth Minister By Education

Highest Degree	High School	Associate	Bachelor	Master	Doctorate
Number Of Respondents	32	10	239	113	7
Salary (100%*)	22,451	23,702	26,155	31,448	31,772
Annual % Increase (71%)	6%	5%	5%	6%	3%
Parsonage (9%)	16,269	0	8,858	11,623	0
Housing (66%)	15,286	19,472	16,985	17,275	12,348
Retirement (55%)	2,655	2,340	2,628	3,398	4,405
Life Insurance (35%)	192	372	385	557	62
Health Insurance (77%)	7,014	8,565	6,090	6,287	7,450
Vacation/weeks (95%)	3	3	3	3	3
Education Funds (41%)	906	1,233	1,318	1,335	1,933
Auto Allowance (89%)	91%	90%	88%	90%	100%

* The percentage following each compensation item indicates the portion of church administrators who received that form of compensation. The averages in each column are for those individuals who actually received that compensation item. See Chapter 3 for a full explanation of how to read this table.

Total Compensation Comparisons

Highest Degree	High School	Associate	Bachelor	Master	Doctorate
Average attendance	1,003	550	883	865	491
Average church income	1,015,173	944,229	1,171,640	1,722,051	940,892
Average years employed	4	2	4	5	5
Average compensation*	43,044	43,852	44,574	53,486	51,406
Standard deviation	16,885	12,518	13,716	14,475	14,019
Median compensation	39,985	40,500	42,240	51,470	47,559

National Average for all Youth Ministers: $47,058 with a standard deviation of $14,492 (see Chapter 4, Table 4-3).

Total respondents: 401

* includes base salary, housing or parsonage allowance, retirement contribution, life and health insurance payments, and educational funds.

Table 8-7: Annual Compensation Of Youth Minister By Years Employed

Years Employed	0-5	6-10	11-15	over 15
Number Of Respondents	350	84	23	7
Salary 100(%*)	26,772	30,058	31,491	35,265
Annual % Increase (71%)	5%	5%	6%	6%
Parsonage (9%)	11,605	9,989	9,500	15,000
Housing (66%)	16,109	20,603	17,130	23,250
Retirement (55%)	2,654	3,146	3,222	4,128
Life Insurance (35%)	502	309	178	1,220
Health Insurance (77%)	6,057	7,369	8,176	6,466
Vacation/weeks (95%)	3	3	3	4
Education Funds (41%)	1,138	1,816	1,571	2,167
Auto Allowance (89%)	88%	95%	83%	100%

* The percentage following each compensation item indicates the portion of church administrators who received that form of compensation. The averages in each column are for those individuals who actually received that compensation item. See Chapter 3 for a full explanation of how to read this table.

Total Compensation Comparisons

Years Employed	0-5	6-10	11-15	Over 15
Average attendance	784	1,069	1,053	1,545
Average church income	1,122,829	1,711,143	1,903,702	3,324,432
Average years employed	2	7	12	19
Average compensation*	44,736	53,740	56,386	67,119
Standard deviation	13,231	15,005	14,374	21,758
Median compensation	43,687	50,374	54,583	65,804

National Average for all Youth Ministers: $47,058 with a standard deviation of $14,492 (see Chapter 4, Table 4-3).

Total respondents: 464

* includes base salary, housing or parsonage allowance, retirement contribution, life and health insurance payments, and educational funds.

Table 8-8: Annual Compensation Of Part-Time Youth Ministers By Hours Worked

Hours-per-week	1-14	15-29	30-39	All Part-time
Number Of Respondents	7	18	4	91
Salary (100%*)	7,412	12,014	16,625	11,643
Annual % Increase (41%)	3%	5%	2%	4%
Parsonage (2%)	0	0	0	2,000
Housing (11%)	0	10,708	12,000	8,602
Retirement (9%)	0	4,930	2,750	2,461
Life Insurance (0%)	0	0	0	0
Health Insurance (5%)	0	6,779	7,200	6,200
Vacation/weeks (47%)	2	2	2	2
Education Funds (20%)	305	520	0	1,112
Auto Allowance (66%)	71%	94%	75%	66%

* The percentage following each compensation item indicates the portion of part-time church administrators who received that form of compensation. The averages in each column are for those individuals who actually received that compensation item. See Chapter 3 for a full explanation of how to read this table.

Total Compensation Comparisons

Hours Worked Per Week	1-14	15-29	30-39	All Part-time
Average attendance	192	835	310	340
Average church income	312,300	691,188	472,789	438,214
Average years employed	3	3	2	3
Average hours per week	9	20	30	19
Average compensation	7,499	14,593	22,112	13,410
Ave. hourly compensation*	16.02	14.03	14.17	13.57
Average hourly salary**	15.84	11.55	10.66	11.78

Total respondents: 91

* includes base salary, housing or parsonage allowance, retirement contribution, life and health insurance payments, and educational funds.

** includes base salary only; see discussion of "rounding errors" in Chapter 3.

Chapter 9

Choir and Music Directors

Employment Profile

A significant percentage of music and choir directors serve on a part-time basis. While men occupy most of the full-time positions, part-time positions divide about equally between males and females. Choir and music directors provided the following employment profile:

	Full-time	Part-time
❏ Number of Respondents	323	301
❏ Ordained	59%	8%
❏ Average years employed	7	6
❏ Male	83%	46%
❏ Female	17%	54%
❏ Self-employed	1%	4%
❏ Church Employee	99%	96%
❏ High School Diploma	9%	12%
❏ Associate's Degree	2%	3%
❏ Bachelor's Degree	42%	53%
❏ Master's Degree	44%	27%
❏ Doctorate	3%	5%

Compensation Analysis

The analysis below is based upon the tables found later in this chapter. The tables present compensation data according to worship attendance, church income, combinations of size and setting, gender, education, and years employed for music and choir directors who serve full-time. The final table provides data for part-time music and choir directors based upon the number of hours worked. In this way, the compensation of music and choir directors can be viewed from a variety of useful perspectives. The total compensation amount found in a separate box at the bottom of each page includes the base salary, housing or parsonage amount, life and health insurance payments, retirement contribution, and educational funds.

Key Points

✎ *Compensation increases steadily with church size.* While music and choir directors start out low, they experience one of the fastest rate of increases of all staff positions. The greatest gains occurred when the attendance reached 200, and then increases sreadily after that. *See Table 9-1.*

✎ *Church income impacted compensation in a pattern similar to church attendance.* Again, compensation started off low, but increased rapidly. The vast majority of choir directors work in churches with an annual income over $1,000,000. These individuals receive, on average, over $20,000 a year more compensation than choir directors in churches with an annual income under $500,000. *See Table 9-2.*

✎ *Over the past several years, compensation has fluctuated by geographical setting in smaller congregations.* This year the highest level of compensation was found in churches located in medium size cities. In previous years, urban and suburban churches provided the highest compensation for smaller congregations under 500 in attendance. Churches with an attendance under 500 provided a compensation package below the national average. *See Table 9-3.*

✎ *Larger churches, except those in rural settings, tend to be above or near the national average, regardless of geographical setting.* Urban, suburban, and churches in medium size cities provided the highest levels of compensation, with urban churches providing higher salaries. Yet all the churches in this category (other than rural) were above the national average. *See Table 9-4.*

✎ *Male directors earned considerably more than did female directors.* On average, females earned 73% of the compensation of their male counterparts. The actual salary difference between men and women was less than $1,000, but fewer females received fringe benefits. Also, few women had full-time positions, and those that did tended to work in congregations with lower budgets. Gender, however, is the key variable affecting compensation. *See Table 9-5.*

✎ *College graduates received substantially higher compensation than did high school graduates; having a graduate degree tended to increase the compensation above the national average.* College graduates earned over $7,000 more than those with a high school education. This year, as in previous years, significant increases occurred for those having a master's or a doctoral degree. As a group, they tend to be the only ones above the national average, although this year those with doctoral degrees were slightly below the national average. *See Table 9-6.*

✎ *Length of employment had some impact upon compensation levels.* Those with less than five years of service received a compensation below the national average. This represented 56% of all music and choir directors. Compensation rose slowly with years of service. *See Table 9-7.*

✎ *Most part-time directors work about 15 hours or less per week.* Historically, more music and choir directors serve part-time than full-time. Hourly compensation was the highest for those working the fewest hours per week. *See Table 9-8.*

Benefits

Full-time staff members. Most fringe benefits were comparable to those of other professional staff members. Few received a parsonage allowance, although 57% did receive a housing allowance.

Part-time staff members. Part-time workers receive few benefits, but they generally work only about 15 hours per week.

Benefits Part-time	Full-time	Part-time
☐ Housing allowance	57%	2%
☐ Parsonage provided	4%	0%
☐ Retirement	59%	4%
☐ Life insurance	36%	2%
☐ Health insurance	76%	5%
☐ Paid vacation	95%	43%
☐ Auto allowance	89%	65%
☐ Continuing education funds	39%	15%

Eleven Year Compensation Trend: National Average for Music and Choir Directors

☐	1993	$38,887
☐	1994	$40,178
☐	1995	$40,701
☐	1996	$43,790
☐	1997	$43,598
☐	1998	$45,603
☐	1999	$49,383
☐	2000	$50,911
☐	2001	$53,200
☐	2002	$55,046
☐	2003	$56,875

Table 9-1: Annual Compensation Of Music or Choir Director By Worship Attendance

Church Attendance	0-99	100-299	300-499	500-749	750-999	over 1,000
Number Of Respondents	3	33	68	74	53	84
Salary (100%*)	17,223	27,321	31,858	36,794	37,314	41,056
Annual % Increase (70%)	4%	6%	3%	4%	4%	4%
Parsonage (4%)	0	15,000	23,443	13,467	7,900	22,680
Housing (57%)	0	16,454	19,711	22,494	20,554	24,155
Retirement (59%)	0	2,942	3,121	4,055	3,623	3,598
Life Insurance (36%)	0	289	497	765	551	328
Health Insurance (76%)	0	6,167	6,839	7,365	6,912	6,617
Vacation/weeks (95%)	4	3	3	3	3	3
Education Funds (39%)	0	1,193	894	1,130	1,243	1,499
Auto Allowance (89%)	33%	76%	90%	92%	87%	95%

* The percentage following each compensation item indicates the portion of all music or choir directors who received that form of compensation. The averages in each column are for those individuals who actually received that compensation item. See Chapter 3 for a full explanation of how to read this table.

Total Compensation Comparisons At A Glance*

Worship Attendance	0-99	100-299	300-499	500-749	750-999	over 1000
Average attendance	77	218	383	611	860	2,137
Average church income	183,037	413,402	839,582	1,219,755	1,746,918	3,080,453
Average years employed	9	6	6	7	7	8
Average compensation*	17,223	42,177	51,209	57,094	56,953	68,207
Standard deviation	16,981	16,334	14,125	17,332	14,468	20,705
Median compensation	6,100	42,220	52,506	53,900	58,789	65,999

National average: $56,875 with a standard deviation of $19,354 (see Chapter 4, Table 4-3)

Total respondents: 315

* includes base salary, housing or parsonage allowance, retirement contribution, life and health insurance payments, and educational funds.

Table 9-2: Annual Compensation Of Music or Choir Director By Church Budget

Church Budget in $	0-249,999	250,000-499,999	500,000-749,000	750,000-999,999	1,000,000 +
Number Of Respondents	12	30	34	44	178
Salary (100%*)	25,646	25,507	32,838	33,165	39,932
Annual % Increase (70%)	3%	6%	4%	3%	4%
Parsonage (4%)	0	10,400	19,167	24,960	16,033
Housing (57%)	21,866	16,836	19,520	22,384	22,631
Retirement (59%)	3,308	2,428	3,330	2,951	3,849
Life Insurance (36%)	353	318	457	239	537
Health Insurance (76%)	6,789	5,165	6,872	6,995	7,000
Vacation/weeks (95%)	3	3	3	3	3
Education Funds (39%)	740	1,072	1,123	863	1,300
Auto Allowance (89%)	67%	73%	88%	89%	92%

* The percentage following each compensation item indicates the portion of all music or choir directors who received that form of compensation. The averages in each column are for those individuals who actually received that compensation item. See Chapter 3 for a full explanation of how to read this table.

Total Compensation Comparisons

Church Budget	0-249,999	250,000-499,999	500,000-749,999	750,000-999,999	1,000,000+
Average attendance	428	241	405	523	1,353
Average church income	149,229	365,633	632,580	869,979	2,283,037
Average years employed	9	5	6	7	8
Average compensation*	41,043	40,432	49,155	52,215	63,542
Standard deviation	26,743	13,673	14,767	13,638	18,490
Median compensation	41,751	39,500	48,150	50,700	61,421

National average: $56,875 with a standard deviation of $19,354 (see Chapter 4, Table 4-3)

Total respondents: 298

* includes base salary, housing or parsonage allowance, retirement contribution, life and health insurance payments, and educational funds.

Table 9-3: Annual Compensation Of Music/Choir Director By Church Setting And Size

Attendance Under 500	Urban	Suburban	Medium City	Small Town	Rural
Number Of Respondents	13	37	21	25	5
Salary (100%*)	37,875	27,349	30,293	29,846	30,287
Annual % Increase (70%)	3%	5%	3%	3%	7%
Parsonage (4%)	0	19,167	19,240	0	0
Housing (57%)	20,435	20,815	17,000	18,537	15,700
Retirement (59%)	4,073	2,152	3,397	3,556	2,802
Life Insurance (36%)	1,351	325	141	465	175
Health Insurance (76%)	5,426	6,365	9,081	6,663	6,003
Vacation/weeks (95%)	4	3	3	3	2
Education Funds (39%)	1,231	895	1,028	925	500
Auto Allowance (89%)	100%	81%	100%	68%	80%

* The percentage following each compensation item indicates the portion of all music or choir directors who received that form of compensation. The averages in each column are for those individuals who actually received that compensation item. See Chapter 3 for a full explanation of how to read this table.

Total Compensation Comparisons

Attendance Under 500	Urban	Suburban	Medium City	Small Town	Rural
Average attendance	332	315	320	338	236
Average church income	989,428	640,631	648,861	670,977	417,127
Average years employed	7	5	6	7	3
Average compensation*	49,923	46,482	50,971	44,154	44,061
Standard deviation	15,067	46,482	16,631	15,713	5,885
Median compensation	49,600	17,957	49,152	45,633	42,220

National average: $56,875 with a standard deviation of $19,354 (see Chapter 4, Table 4-3)

Total respondents: 101

* includes base salary, housing or parsonage allowance, retirement contribution, life and health insurance payments, and educational funds.

Table 9-4: Annual Compensation Of Music/Choir Director By Church Setting And Size

Attendance Over 499	Urban	Suburban	Medium City	Small Town	Rural
Number Of Respondents	36	88	57	22	6
Salary (100%*)	44,983	39,474	37,335	31,738	29,350
Annual % Increase (70%)	4%	4%	5%	4%	6%
Parsonage (4%)	0	21,400	17,367	1,200	0
Housing (57%)	26,807	24,584	21,076	19,944	15,834
Retirement (59%)	4,293	3,740	3,259	3,916	4,216
Life Insurance (36%)	248	698	312	431	750
Health Insurance (76%)	6,509	6,981	7,124	7,287	6,246
Vacation/weeks (95%)	3	3	3	3	3
Education Funds (39%)	1,281	1,294	1,359	1,243	1,000
Auto Allowance (89%)	89%	93%	93%	86%	100%

* The percentage following each compensation item indicates the portion of all music or choir directors who received that form of compensation. The averages in each column are for those individuals who actually received that compensation item. See Chapter 3 for a full explanation of how to read this table.

Total Compensation Comparisons

Attendance Over 499	Urban	Suburban	Medium City	Small Town	Rural
Average attendance	1,491	1,350	1,272	855	920
Average church income	2,705,476	2,276,004	1,692,863	1,613,910	1,063,833
Average years employed	7	8	7	5	7
Average compensation*	64,852	63,687	60,084	57,181	45,934
Standard deviation	23,517	18,517	16,114	16,872	16,571
Median compensation	62,524	62,316	59,722	55,962	37,316

National average: $56,875 with a standard deviation of $19,354 (see Chapter 4, Table 4-3)

Total respondents: 209

* includes base salary, housing or parsonage allowance, retirement contribution, life and health insurance payments, and educational funds.

Table 9-5: Annual Compensation Of Music or Choir Director By Gender

Gender	Male	Female
Number Of Respondents	265	55
Salary (100%*)	36,039	35,115
Annual % Increase (70%)	4%	6%
Parsonage (4%)	17,662	22,200
Housing (57%)	21,742	22,092
Retirement (59%)	3,546	3,615
Life Insurance (36%)	495	355
Health Insurance (76%)	7,174	5,104
Vacation/weeks (95%)	3	3
Education Funds (39%)	1,167	1,052
Auto Allowance (89%)	88%	91%

* The percentage following each compensation item indicates the portion of all music or choir directors who received that form of compensation. The averages in each column are for those individuals who actually received that compensation item. See Chapter 3 for a full explanation of how to read this table.

Total Compensation Comparisons

Gender	Male	Female
Averahe attendance	1,000	827
Average church income	1,700,771	1,213,249
Average years employed	7	7
Average compensation*	59,549	43,684
Standard deviation	18,779	16,822
Median compensation	58,324	43,859

National average: $56,875 with a standard deviation of $19,354 (see Chapter 4, Table 4-3)

Total respondents: 320

* includes base salary, housing or parsonage allowance, retirement contribution, life and health insurance payments, and educational funds.

Table 9-6: Annual Compensation Of Music or Choir Director By Education

Highest Degree	High School	Associate	Bachelor	Master	Doctorate
Number Of Respondents	25	6	116	119	8
Salary (100%*)	30,327	23,393	33,005	39,550	37,608
Annual % Increase (70%)	8%	5%	4%	5%	3%
Parsonage (4%)	0	0	16,425	14,131	25,000
Housing (57%)	20,748	15,300	22,227	21,626	22,500
Retirement (59%)	2,244	1,900	3.036	4,056	2,328
Life Insurance (36%)	418	174	395	468	208
Health Insurance (76%)	6,224	4,453	6,698	7,254	6,911
Vacation/weeks (95%)	3	3	3	3	4
Education Funds (39%)	833	500	1,102	1,250	967
Auto Allowance (89%)	88%	83%	92%	88%	88%

* The percentage following each compensation item indicates the portion of all music or choir directors who received that form of compensation. The averages in each column are for those individuals who actually received that compensation item. See Chapter 3 for a full explanation of how to read this table.

Total Compensation Comparisons

Highest Degree	High School	Associate	Bachelor	Master	Doctorate
Average attendance	899	574	983	1,010	914
Average church income	1,080,834	1,016,885	1,602,774	1,751,946	1,905,395
Average years employed	6	4	5	9	6
Average compensation*	47,196	36,911	54,408	62,545	53,411
Standard deviation	15,512	8,942	17,661	19,235	28,755
Median compensation	45,000	36,860	51,500	61,078	46,075

National average: $56,875 with a standard deviation of $19,354 (see Chapter 4, Table 4-3)

Total respondents: 274

* includes base salary, housing or parsonage allowance, retirement contribution, life and health insurance payments, and educational funds.

Table 9-7: Annual Compensation Of Music or Choir Director By Years Employed

Years Employed	0-5	6-10	11-15	over 15
Number Of Respondents	176	68	30	39
Salary (100%*)	34,960	35,138	34,772	41,189
Annual % Increase (70%)	5%	4%	5%	4%
Parsonage (4%)	19,595	18,924	0	13,500
Housing (57%)	20,924	21,085	23,679	24,133
Retirement (59%)	3,323	3,169	3,214	4,674
Life Insurance (36%)	391	746	412	507
Health Insurance (76%)	6,213	7,858	6,620	8,150
Vacation/weeks (95%)	3	3	4	4
Education Funds (39%)	1,191	993	858	1,263
Auto Allowance (89%)	90%	94%	77%	92%

* The percentage following each compensation item indicates the portion of all music or choir directors who received that form of compensation. The averages in each column are for those individuals who actually received that compensation item. See Chapter 3 for a full explanation of how to read this table.

Total Compensation Comparisons

Years Employed	0-5	6-10	11-15	over 15
Average attendance	947	979	1,001	1,064
Average church income	1,499,183	1,694,216	1,488,947	2,013,762
Average years employed	3	8	12	21
Average compensation*	53,767	57,887	56,557	67,341
Standard deviation	16,540	22,151	21,945	20,549
Median compensation	52,300	57,288	58,789	65,634

National average: $56,875 with a standard deviation of $19,354 (see Chapter 4, Table 4-3)

Total respondents: 313

* includes base salary, housing or parsonage allowance, retirement contribution, life and health insurance payments, and educational funds.

Table 9-8: Annual Compensation Of Part-Time Music/Choir Directors By Hrs. Worked

Hours-per-week	1-14	15-29	30-39	All Part-time
Number Of Respondents	58	57	12	301
Salary (99%*)	10,988	16,426	26,172	13,055
Annual % Increase (58%)	4%	4%	4%	5%
Parsonage (0%)	0	0	0	0
Housing (2%)	0	9,424	0	8,491
Retirement (4%)	0	1,308	841	1,171
Life Insurance (2%)	0	72	100	149
Health Insurance (5%)	4,482	3,040	5,176	4,363
Vacation/weeks (43%)	3	2	3	3
Education Funds (15%)	279	469	556	484
Auto Allowance (65%)	79%	82%	92%	65%

* The percentage following each compensation item indicates the portion of all part-time music or choir directors who received that form of compensation. The averages in each column are for those individuals who actually received that compensation item. See Chapter 3 for a full explanation of how to read this table.

Total Compensation Comparisons

Hours Worked Per Week	1-14	15-29	30-39	All Part-time
Average attendance	280	999	467	446
Average church income	431,315	816,699	837,361	506,600
Average years employed	6	6	9	6
Average hours per week	8	19	32	15
Average compensation	11,101	17,075	28,161	13,530
Ave. hourly compensation**	26.69	17.28	16.92	17.35
Average hourly salary*	26.41	16.63	15.73	16.74

Total respondents: 301

* includes base salary, housing or parsonage allowance, retirement contribution, life and health insurance payments, and educational funds.

* includes base salary only; see discussion on "rounding errors" in Chapter 3.

Chapter 10

Church Administrators

Employment Profile

Church administrators tend to serve in larger churches. In this study, 25% of those working full-time were ordained ministers, although this percentage declines significantly for those serving part-time. Men hold a majority of the full-time positions while women are in a majority for those working part-time. This group of administrators provided the following employment profile:

	Full-time	Part-time
Number of Respondents	345	88
Ordained	25%	10%
Average years employed	7	6
Male	59%	39%
Female	41%	61%
Self-employed	1%	1%
Church Employee	99%	99%
High School Diploma	17%	19%
Associate's Degree	8%	8%
Bachelor's Degree	40%	46%
Master's Degree	32%	27%
Doctorate	3%	0%

Compensation Analysis

The analysis below is based upon the tables found later in this chapter. The tables present compensation data according to worship attendance, church income, combinations of size and setting, gender, education, and years employed for administrators who serve full-time. The final table provides data for part-time administrators based upon the number of hours worked. In this way, the administrator's compensation can be viewed from a variety of useful perspectives. The total compensation amount found in a separate box at the bottom of each page includes the base salary, housing or parsonage amount, life and health insurance payments, retirement contribution, and educational funds.

Key Points

✎ *Compensation increased with church size.* Base salary and total compensation increased with church size. Business administrators most often worked in larger churches. Over 60% worked in churches with an attendance over 500. About 25% worked in churches over 1,000. The national average compensation corresponded to an attendance of between 600-700. *See Table 10-1.*

✎ *Church budget had a direct impact on compensation.* Generally, compensation increased as church income increased. Over half of the administrators participating in this study worked in churches with income over $1,000,000. *See Table 10-2.*

✎ *Urban and suburban churches tend to provid the highest compensation for smaller congregations.* Few rural churches employ business administrators, although this year their income was among the highest for this group of churches. On average, business administrators in congregations with an attendance under 500 tended to receive compensation levels below the national average regardless of the church's geographical setting. *See Table 10-3.*

✎ *Urban and suburban churches tend to provid the highest compensation for larger churches (attendance above 500).* About 25% of administrators in this group work in suburban churches. Those serving in rural settings and small towns earn considerably less than their urban and suburban counterparts. *See Table 10-4.*

✎ *On average, male church business administrators received over $20,000 more compensation than did females.* On average, females earned 63% of their male counterparts. This represented the largest earning gap of any church staff position. In terms of salary alone, women earned about $10,000 per year less. Women earned below the national average even though they served in churches with incomes and attendances that should have reflected higher compensation levels. *See Table 10-5.*

✎ *College graduates received substantially higher compensation than did high school graduates; having a graduate degree increased the compensation.* College graduates earned about $10,000 more than those with only a high school education. Significant increases occurred over the national average once the administrator earned a graduate degree. *See Table 10-6.*

✎ *Length of employment had no significant impact upon compensation levels.* Those serving on average 13 years earned less than the national average. Fifty-seven percent of church business administrators had worked for their church an average of three years. *See Table 10-7.*

✎ *Most part-time administrators work about 24 hours per week.* On average, they earn significantly less per hour than a full-time administrator. This is due to the decreased levels of compensation provided to the increased number of female part-time administrators. *See Table 10-8.*

Benefits

Full-time staff members. Most fringe benefits were slightly less than those of other professional staff members. Fewer church business administrators received housing or parsonage allowances reflecting the mixed ministerial status of this group.

Part-time staff members. Twenty percent of the church business administrators surveyed worked part-time. Females comprised over half of this group.

Benefits Part-time	Full-time	Part-time
☐ Housing allowance	22%	5%
☐ Parsonage provided	2%	1%
☐ Retirement	53%	17%
☐ Life insurance	32%	7%
☐ Health insurance	63%	18%
☐ Paid vacation	92%	62%
☐ Auto allowance	84%	82%
☐ Continuing education funds	33%	20%

Eleven Year Compensation Trend: National Averages for Church Administrators

☐	1993	$35,333
☐	1994	$37,865
☐	1995	$36,225
☐	1996	$36,871
☐	1997	$37,413
☐	1998	$40,207
☐	1999	$42,277
☐	2000	$44,768
☐	2001	$48,064
☐	2002	$47,305
☐	2003	$50,615

Table 10-1: Annual Compensation Of Administrator By Worship Attendance

Church Attendance	0-99	100-299	300-499	500-749	750-999	over 1000
Number Of Respondents	4	56	61	75	51	85
Salary (100%*)	22,584	27,348	32,828	38,151	45,117	48,840
Annual % Increase (72%)	3%	5%	4%	5%	4%	6%
Parsonage (2%)	0	0	23,600	15,750	9,750	18,000
Housing (22%)	0	16,582	21,190	21,631	21,588	26,658
Retirement (53%)	0	3,503	2,765	3,426	3,423	3,801
Life Insurance (32%)	0	506	776	964	1,204	380
Health Insurance (63%)	0	5,881	5,357	6,251	7,131	6,302
Vacation/weeks (92%)	3	3	3	3	3	3
Education Funds (33%)	0	369	860	1,475	1,497	1,477
Auto Allowance (84%)	50%	68%	93%	87%	88%	88%

* The percentage following each compensation item indicates the portion of church administrators who received that form of compensation. The averages in each column are for those individuals who actually received that compensation item. See Chapter 3 for a full explanation of how to read this table.

Total Compensation Comparisons At A Glance*

Worship Attendance	0-99	100-299	300-499	500-749	750-999	over 1000
Average attendance	78	191	383	611	850	2,661
Average church income	152,667	368,172	848,352	1,238,537	1,765,381	3,174,754
Average years employed	2	7	6	7	6	7
Average compensation*	22,584	33,221	41,956	48,938	56,458	68,294
Standard deviation	11,940	13,459	14,298	15,913	15,870	18,179
Median compensation	15,600	30,320	39,232	48,105	54,227	66,195

National average for all Administrators: $50,615 with a standard deviation of $19,939 (see Chapter 4, Table 4-3)

Total respondents: 332

* includes base salary, housing or parsonage allowance, retirement contribution, life and health insurance payments, and educational funds.

Table 10-2: Annual Compensation Of Administrator By Church Budget

Church Budget in $	0-249,999	250,000-499,999	500,000-749,000	750,000-999,999	1,000,000 +
Number Of Respondents	14	42	31	41	180
Salary (100%*)	29,150	27,630	32,716	33,169	45,240
Annual % Increase (72%)	6%	4%	6%	4%	5%
Parsonage (2%)	0	0	0	19,300	12,000
Housing (22%)	5,200	18,428	16,314	20,225	25,574
Retirement (53%)	3,678	2,799	2,483	3,247	3,714
Life Insurance (32%)	462	367	721	195	788
Health Insurance (63%)	6,742	5,625	5,522	6,032	6,517
Vacation/weeks (92%)	3	3	3	3	3
Education Funds (33%)	550	426	1,061	838	1,532
Auto Allowance (84%)	43%	74%	81%	90%	90%

* The percentage following each compensation item indicates the portion of church administrators who received that form of compensation. The averages in each column are for those individuals who actually received that compensation item. See Chapter 3 for a full explanation of how to read this table.

Total Compensation Comparisons

Church Budget	0-249,999	250,000-499,999	500,000-749,999	750,000-999,999	1,000,000+
Average attendance	274	243	427	590	1,581
Average church income	188,384	344,785	611,934	860,316	2,344,615
Average years employed	8	6	7	7	7
Average compensation*	34,495	33,417	41,800	41,973	61,064
Standard deviation	16,428	13,764	12,076	12,177	18,802
Median compensation	30,050	31,204	41,800	40,000	61,055

National average for all Administrators: $50,615 with a standard deviation of $19,939 (see Chapter 4, Table 4-3)

Total respondents: 308

* includes base salary, housing or parsonage allowance, retirement contribution, life and health insurance payments, and educational funds.

Table 10-3: Annual Compensation Of Administrator By Church Setting And Size

Attendance Under 500	Urban	Suburban	Medium City	Small Town	Rural
Number Of Respondents	22	43	24	22	7
Salary (100%*)	35,425	30,487	27,844	25,447	28,089
Annual % Increase (72%)	4%	5%	4%	4%	7%
Parsonage (2%)	0	23,600	0	0	0
Housing (22%)	22,256	21,725	13,760	23,300	24,000
Retirement (53%)	4,014	2,802	2,753	2,510	3,300
Life Insurance (32%)	1,600	308	542	116	0
Health Insurance (63%)	5,145	6,354	4,884	4,601	8,310
Vacation/weeks (92%)	3	3	3	3	3
Education Funds (33%)	831	745	430	400	483
Auto Allowance (84%)	91%	91%	71%	68%	57%

* The percentage following each compensation item indicates the portion of church administrators who received that form of compensation. The averages in each column are for those individuals who actually received that compensation item. See Chapter 3 for a full explanation of how to read this table.

Total Compensation Comparisons

Attendance Under 500	Urban	Suburban	Medium City	Small Town	Rural
Average attendance	294	293	272	275	288
Average church income	736,082	630,871	632,510	516,339	461,106
Average years employed	5	6	7	6	7
Average compensation*	43,103	37,574	35,095	31,250	38,132
Standard deviation	15,963	13,240	14,906	14,926	9,332
Median compensation	38,150	34,000	33,300	28,740	31,971

National average for all Administrators: $50,615 with a standard deviation of $19,939 (see Chapter 4, Table 4-3)

Total respondents: 118

* includes base salary, housing or parsonage allowance, retirement contribution, life and health insurance payments, and educational funds.

Table 10-4: Annual Compensation Of Administrator By Church Setting And Size

Attendance Over 499	Urban	Suburban	Medium City	Small Town	Rural
Number Of Respondents	36	88	54	27	5
Salary (100%*)	48,887	45,838	42,134	39,167	31,356
Annual % Increase (72%)	6%	5%	5%	5%	3%
Parsonage (2%)	0	16,500	13,125	0	0
Housing (22%)	27,442	27,594	22,851	19,950	13,500
Retirement (53%)	4,363	3,806	2,884	3,473	0
Life Insurance (32%)	327	1,123	242	611	50
Health Insurance (63%)	6,792	6,302	6,541	6,288	9,142
Vacation/weeks (92%)	3	4	3	3	3
Education Funds (33%)	1,440	1,764	1.155	1,100	1,733
Auto Allowance (84%)	83%	88%	87%	93%	100%

* The percentage following each compensation item indicates the portion of church administrators who received that form of compensation. The averages in each column are for those individuals who actually received that compensation item. See Chapter 3 for a full explanation of how to read this table.

Total Compensation Comparisons

Attendance Over 499	Urban	Suburban	Medium City	Small Town	Rural
Average attendance	2,183	1,583	1,299	825	895
Average church income	2,932,217	2,403,789	1,651,141	1,514,693	1,124,000
Average years employed	6	7	7	6	7
Average compensation*	63,767	60,314	58,173	50,348	43,291
Standard deviation	20,656	18,788	15,689	19,463	15,361
Median compensation	61,000	61,009	56,400	47,165	34,089

National average for all Administrators: $50,615 with a standard deviation of $19,939 (see Chapter 4, Table 4-3)

Total respondents: 210

* includes base salary, housing or parsonage allowance, retirement contribution, life and health insurance payments, and educational funds.

Table 10-5: Annual Compensation Of Administrator By Gender

Gender	Male	Female
Number Of Respondents	202	143
Salary (100%*)	42,913	32,912
Annual % Increase (72%)	5%	5%
Parsonage (2%)	15,433	0
Housing (22%)	23,247	24,000
Retirement (53%)	3,703	2,974
Life Insurance (32%)	632	732
Health Insurance (63%)	6,588	5,495
Vacation/weeks (92%)	3	3
Education Funds (33%)	1,404	894
Auto Allowance (84%)	90%	76%

* The percentage following each compensation item indicates the portion of church administrators who received that form of compensation. The averages in each column are for those individuals who actually received that compensation item. See Chapter 3 for a full explanation of how to read this table.

Total Compensation Comparisons

Gender	Male	Female
Averahe attendance	1,264	749
Average church income	1,951,077	1,054,912
Average years employed	6	8
Average compensation*	59,898	37,504
Standard deviation	17,760	14,864
Median compensation	57,873	34,976

National average for all Administrators: $50,615 with a standard deviation of $19,939 (see Chapter 4, Table 4-3)

Total respondents: 345

* includes base salary, housing or parsonage allowance, retirement contribution, life and health insurance payments, and educational funds.

Table 10-6: Annual Compensation Of Administrator By Education

Highest Degree	High School	Associate	Bachelor	Master	Doctorate
Number Of Respondents	48	23	109	86	7
Salary (100%*)	32,531	35,537	39,986	43,354	32,611
Annual % Increase (72%)	4%	6%	5%	4%	3%
Parsonage (2%)	15,000	0	23,600	10,000	0
Housing (22%)	19,514	24,500	23,685	24,908	24,380
Retirement (53%)	2,471	2,768	3,385	4,076	2,766
Life Insurance (32%)	220	634	337	781	263
Health Insurance (63%)	6,384	4,805	6,169	6,476	5,854
Vacation/weeks (92%)	3	4	3	3	3
Education Funds (33%)	743	1,038	1,330	1,278	1,200
Auto Allowance (84%)	81%	74%	84%	92%	71%

* The percentage following each compensation item indicates the portion of church administrators who received that form of compensation. The averages in each column are for those individuals who actually received that compensation item. See Chapter 3 for a full explanation of how to read this table.

Total Compensation Comparisons

Highest Degree	High School	Associate	Bachelor	Master	Doctorate
Average attendance	1,025	1,867	1,009	1,045	980
Average church income	1,009,793	1,781,922	1,553,501	2,061,752	1,733,646
Average years employed	7	10	7	6	4
Average compensation*	40,829	44,752	50,792	59,758	57,304
Standard deviation	18,656	19,687	17,572	22,046	17,625
Median compensation	36,200	45,822	48,000	56,213	52,404

National average for all Administrators: $50,615 with a standard deviation of $19,939 (see Chapter 4, Table 4-3)

Total respondents: 273

* includes base salary, housing or parsonage allowance, retirement contribution, life and health insurance payments, and educational funds.

Table 10-7: Annual Compensation Of Administrator By Years Employed

Years Employed	0-5	6-10	11-15	over 15
Number Of Respondents	194	72	38	38
Salary (100%*)	38,733	39,056	34,992	40,729
Annual % Increase (72%)	5%	6%	5%	3%
Parsonage (2%)	15,033	15,750	16,000	0
Housing (22%)	21,838	25,338	21,811	28,531
Retirement (53%)	3,369	3,230	3,418	3,971
Life Insurance (32%)	452	1,004	849	619
Health Insurance (63%)	6,450	5,961	5,543	6,046
Vacation/weeks (92%)	3	3	4	4
Education Funds (33%)	1,177	1,403	762	1,253
Auto Allowance (84%)	85%	89%	76%	82%

* The percentage following each compensation item indicates the portion of church administrators who received that form of compensation. The averages in each column are for those individuals who actually received that compensation item. See Chapter 3 for a full explanation of how to read this table.

Total Compensation Comparisons

Years Employed	0-5	6-10	11-15	over 15
Average attendance	1,161	833	1,108	915
Average church income	1,658,680	1,508,177	1,528,054	1,620,565
Average years employed	3	7	13	20
Average compensation*	50,060	51,579	46,715	54,126
Standard deviation	18,521	21,564	20,961	22,715
Median compensation	49,590	48,000	37,754	49,584

National average for all Administrators: $50,615 with a standard deviation of $19,939 (see Chapter 4, Table 4-3)

Total respondents: 342

* includes base salary, housing or parsonage allowance, retirement contribution, life and health insurance payments, and educational funds.

Table 10-8: Annual Compensation Of Part-Time Administrators By Hours Worked

Hours-per-week	1-14	15-29	30-39	All Part-time
Number Of Respondents	5	24	21	88
Salary (100%*)	7,756	18,085	26,507	19,428
Annual % Increase (64%)	36%	3%	7%	6%
Parsonage (1%)	0	0	0	10,000
Housing (5%)	0	0	17,750	16,489
Retirement (17%)	0	1,302	1,957	2,104
Life Insurance (7%)	0	0	554	419
Health Insurance (18%)	0	2,735	5,072	4,497
Vacation/weeks (62%)	0	3	3	3
Education Funds (20%)	750	550	222	373
Auto Allowance (82%)	60%	96%	95%	82%

* The percentage following each compensation item indicates the portion of part-time church administrators who received that form of compensation. The averages in each column are for those individuals who actually received that compensation item. See Chapter 3 for a full explanation of how to read this table.

Total Compensation Comparisons

Hours Worked Per Week	1-14	15-29	30-39	All Part-time
Average attendance	124	456	521	384
Average church income	245,006	703,252	723,761	582,739
Average years employed	6	6	6	6
Average hours per week	9	21	32	24
Average compensation	7,906	18,735	30,723	21,573
Ave. hourly compensation**	16.89	17.16	18.46	17.29
Average hourly salary*	16.57	16.56	15.93	15.57

Total respondents: 88

* includes base salary, housing or parsonage allowance, retirement contribution, life and health insurance payments, and educational funds.

* includes base salary only; see discussion on "rounding errors" in Chapter 3.

Chapter 11

Church Bookkeepers

Employment Profile

From an employment standpoint, church bookkeepers are aligned with church secretaries and custodians. Very few are ordained ministers. They tend to be hourly paid church employees with the overwhelming number female, whether full-time or part-time. An increasing number are college graduates. The church bookkeepers surveyed provided the following employment profile:

	Full-time	Part-time
❐ Number of Respondents	199	214
❐ Ordained	2%	0%
❐ Average years employed	8	6
❐ Male	6%	16%
❐ Female	94%	84%
❐ Self-employed	0%	7%
❐ Church Employee	100%	93%
❐ High School Diploma	45%	31%
❐ Associate Degree	21%	16%
❐ Bachelor Degree	31%	46%
❐ Master Degree	3%	7%
❐ Doctorate	0%	0%

Compensation Analysis

The analysis below is based upon the tables found later in this chapter. The tables present compensation data according to worship attendance, church income, combinations of size and setting, gender, education, and years employed for bookkeepers who serve full-time. The final table provides data for part-time bookkeepers based upon the number of hours worked. In this way, the bookkeeper's compensation can be viewed from a variety of useful perspectives. The total compensation amount found in a separate box at the bottom of each page includes the base salary, housing or parsonage amount, life and health insurance payments, retirement contribution, and educational funds.

Key Points

✎ *The compensation of bookkeepers increased significantly in the largest churches.* Total compensation increases with attendance, with the fastest growth occurring once church attendance exceeds 1,000. Over 30% of all church bookkeepers worked in churches of that size or larger. *See Table 11-1.*

✎ *Compensation increased slowly with increases in church income.* About 66% of bookkeepers worked in congregations with an annual income in excess of $1,000,000. The national average compensation was not achieved until the church's income, on average, was over $1,300,000. *See Table 11-2.*

✎ *Urban churches provided the highest compensation for bookkeepers in smaller churches (attendance under 500).* Most curches with an average attendance under 500 provided compensation below the national average. *See Table 11-3.*

✎ *Urban and suburban churches provided the highest compensation for bookkeepers in larger churches (attendance over 500).* In churches with an average attendance over 500, those in small towns, rural settings, and medium size cities were below the national average. *See Table 11-4.*

✎ *Female bookkeepers earned less than did males.* Historically, females have earned less than their male counterparts, although last year they earned slightly more. Men represent only a small percentage of all bookkeepers. This year, females earned about $4,700 less in total compensation. The average compensation for men was above the national average; for women it was slightly below. Both men and women tended to work in larger congregations. *See Table 11-5.*

✎ *Educational achievement had a minor impact on total compensation.* Bookkeepers with college degrees earned slightly more than the national average, while those without a college education tended to earn slightly less. Those with a master's degree, however, earned less than the national average. Yet those with less education had served for longer periods of time. *See Table 11-6.*

✎ *Length of employment had little impact upon the compensation of church bookkeepers.* About half of all full-time bookkeepers had worked an average of three years at their church. These individuals earned earned about 90% as much of the group with an average of 21 years of service. *See Table 11-7.*

✎ *Most part-time bookkeepers work about 19 hours per week.* Historically, their average hourly compensation is higher than that of secretaries and custodians, but less than the other staff positions examined in this study. *See Table 11-8.*

Benefit Analysis

Full-time staff members. Church bookkeepers received less benefits than did administrators or ministerial staff. The percentage of those who received health insurance, retirement contributions, or educational funds was notably less. Only 1% received a housing allowance. Bookkeepers, however, did receive better benefits than secretaries and were about the same as custodians.

Part-time staff members. Over half of the bookkeepers surveyed worked part-time for their churches. The majority worked about 19 hours per week. Over 80% of part-time bookkeepers were women. Part-time bookkeepers earned less than other part-time professional staff, and slightly more than did part-time secretaries or custodians. As with other part-time positions, few received fringe benefits other than a vacation or an auto allowance.

Benefits	Full-time	Part-time
☐ Housing allowance	1%	0%
☐ Parsonage provided	0%	0%
☐ Retirement	41%	9%
☐ Life insurance	35%	4%
☐ Health insurance	60%	5%
☐ Paid vacation	93%	42%
☐ Auto allowance	83%	75%
☐ Continuing education funds	15%	5%

Eleven Year Compensation Trend: National Averages for Bookkeepers

☐	1993	$20,300
☐	1994	$23,172
☐	1995	$22,106
☐	1996	$23,548
☐	1997	$23,839
☐	1998	$24,623
☐	1999	$26,229
☐	2000	$27,992
☐	2001	$29,220
☐	2002	$29,398
☐	2003	$30,457

Table 11-1: Annual Compensation Of Bookkeeper By Worship Attendance

Church Attendance	0-99	100-299	300-499	500-749	750-999	over 1,000
Number Of Respondents	0	16	41	43	31	64
Salary (100%*)		21,349	25,452	26,166	27,868	29,153
Annual % Increase (76%)		8%	3%	4%	4%	5%
Parsonage (0%)		0	0	0	0	0
Housing (1%)		0	0	14,700	0	0
Retirement (41%)		1,087	2,048	1,913	2,258	1,859
Life Insurance (35%)		513	771	438	286	277
Health Insurance (60%)		3,027	4,069	4,356	5,772	4,473
Vacation/weeks (93%)		2	3	3	3	3
Education Funds (15%)		450	400	642	533	503
Auto Allowance (83%)		75%	78%	86%	87%	86%

* The percentage following each compensation item indicates the portion of all church bookkeepers who received that form of compensation. The averages in each column are for those individuals who actually received that compensation item. See Chapter 3 for a full explanation of how to read this table.

Total Compensation Comparisons

Worship Attendance	0-99	100-299	300-499	500-749	750-999	over 1,000
Average attendance		216	390	608	857	2,685
Average church income		488,602	849,428	1,270,291	1,961,850	3,094,942
Average years employed		6	10	6	9	8
Average compensation*		22,993	28,444	30,140	31,934	33,644
Standard deviation		5,782	8,541	7,159	7,376	9,345
Median compensation		21,611	28,463	28,777	31,045	32,733

National average for all bookkeepers: $30,457 with a standard deviation of $8,769 (see Chapter 4, Table 4-3)

Total respondents: 195

* includes base salary, housing or parsonage allowance, retirement contribution, life and health insurance payments, and educational funds.

Table 11-2: Annual Compensation Of Bookkeeper By Church Budget

Church Budget in $	0-249,999	250,000-499,999	500,000-749,000	750,000-999,999	1,000,000 +
Number Of Respondents	7	12	20	22	120
Salary (100%*)	19,288	19,927	22,916	25,590	29,008
Annual % Increase (76%)	4%	7%	3%	4%	5%
Parsonage (0%)	0	0	0	0	0
Housing (1%)	0	0	14,700	0	0
Retirement (41%)	2,560	880	855	1,680	2,173
Life Insurance (35%)	125	0	389	234	428
Health Insurance (60%)	4,236	2,252	4,211	3,868	4,513
Vacation/weeks (93%)	2	2	3	3	3
Education Funds (15%)	350	600	0	258	624
Auto Allowance (83%)	57%	67%	65%	8%2	89%

* The percentage following each compensation item indicates the portion of all church bookkeepers who received that form of compensation. The averages in each column are for those individuals who actually received that compensation item. See Chapter 3 for a full explanation of how to read this table.

Total Compensation Comparisons

Church Budget	0-249,999	250,000-499,999	500,000-749,999	750,000-999,999	1,000,000+
Average attendance	435	292	358	641	1,679
Average church income	153,852	380,919	619,522	870,700	2,390,069
Average years employed	7	4	9	10	8
Average compensation*	20,932	20,687	25,732	28,502	33,377
Standard deviation	8,716	2,889	9,338	6,800	8,279
Median compensation	20,727	20,904	26,189	26,990	32,757

National average for all bookkeepers: $30,457 with a standard deviation of $8,769 (see Chapter 4, Table 4-3)

Total respondents: 181

* includes base salary, housing or parsonage allowance, retirement contribution, life and health insurance payments, and educational funds.

Table 11-3: Annual Compensation Of Bookkeeper By Church Setting And Size

Attendance Under 500	Urban	Suburban	Medium City	Small Town	Rural
Number Of Respondents	4	18	15	15	3
Salary (100%*)	28,659	23,658	25,542	19,276	31,615
Annual % Increase (76%)	3%	3%	8%	3%	2%
Parsonage (0%)	0	0	0	0	0
0Housing (1%)	0	0	0	0	0
Retirement (41%)	3,156	985	1,773	2,291	0
Life Insurance (35%)	256	324	305	0	0
Health Insurance (60%)	2,567	5,039	4,070	2,568	0
Vacation/weeks (93%)	2	3	2	3	3
Education Funds (15%)	600	200	400	350	0
Auto Allowance (83%)	100%	72%	93%	6%0	67%

* The percentage following each compensation item indicates the portion of all church bookkeepers who received that form of compensation. The averages in each column are for those individuals who actually received that compensation item. See Chapter 3 for a full explanation of how to read this table.

Total Compensation Comparisons

Attendance Under 500	Urban	Suburban	Medium City	Small Town	Rural
Average attendance	290	365	309	328	373
Average church income	1,164,250	699,400	731,916	675,239	764,667
Average years employed	8	10	10	8	9
Average compensation*	33,893	26,571	28,771	20,631	31,615
Standard deviation	8,233	8,759	9,156	6,035	8,503
Median compensation	37,364	25,200	28,468	20,771	24,000

National average for all bookkeepers: $30,457 with a standard deviation of $8,769 (see Chapter 4, Table 4-3)

Total respondents: 55

* includes base salary, housing or parsonage allowance, retirement contribution, life and health insurance payments, and educational funds.

Table 11-4: Annual Compensation Of Bookkeeper By Church Setting And Size

Attendance Over 499	Urban	Suburban	Medium City	Small Town	Rural
Number Of Respondents	26	56	41	11	4
Salary (100%*)	27,814	30,509	26,360	23,704	20,404
Annual % Increase (76%)	5%	5%	5%	4%	4%
Parsonage (0%)	0	0	0	0	0
Housing (1%)	0	0	0	14,700	0
Retirement (41%)	2,301	2,010	1,501	2,169	2,550
Life Insurance (35%)	254	336	231	398	1,025
Health Insurance (60%)	5,034	5,175	3,943	4,081	4,064
Vacation/weeks (93%)	3	3	3	3	2
Education Funds (15%)	550	531	670	200	0
Auto Allowance (83%)	85%	86%	85%	91%	100%

* The percentage following each compensation item indicates the portion of all church bookkeepers who received that form of compensation. The averages in each column are for those individuals who actually received that compensation item. See Chapter 3 for a full explanation of how to read this table.

Total Compensation Comparisons

Attendance Over 499	Urban	Suburban	Medium City	Small Town	Rural
Average attendance	2,111	1,920	1,209	779	1,010
Average church income	2,212,653	2,821,932	1,763,924	1,613,358	1,291,250
Average years employed	8	7	8	10	4
Average compensation*	32,336	35,151	29,643	28,750	24,602
Standard deviation	8,822	8,837	7,144	3,644	4,895
Median compensation	33,000	35,136	28,791	26,189	25,267

National average for all bookkeepers: $30,457 with a standard deviation of $8,769 (see Chapter 4, Table 4-3)

Total respondents: 138

* includes base salary, housing or parsonage allowance, retirement contribution, life and health insurance payments, and educational funds.

Table 11-5: Annual Compensation Of Bookkeeper By Gender

Gender	Male	Female
Number Of Respondents	12	187
Salary (100%*)	30,053	26,508
Annual % Increase (76%)	4%	5%
Parsonage (0%)	0	0
Housing (1%)	0	14,700
Retirement (41%)	1,198	1,988
Life Insurance (35%)	226	391
Health Insurance (60%)	5,361	4,378
Vacation/weeks (93%)	3	3
Education Funds (15%)	400	526
Auto Allowance (83%)	67%	84%

* The percentage following each compensation item indicates the portion of all church bookkeepers who received that form of compensation. The averages in each column are for those individuals who actually received that compensation item. See Chapter 3 for a full explanation of how to read this table.

Total Compensation Comparisons

Gender	Male	Female
Average attendance	1,992	1,197
Average church income	2,841,816	1,728,561
Average years employed	6	8
Average compensation*	34,882	30,173
Standard deviation	12,674	8,27
Median compensation	37,855	30,049

National average for all bookkeepers: $30,457 with a standard deviation of $8,769 (see Chapter 4, Table 4-3)

Total respondents: 199

* includes base salary, housing or parsonage allowance, retirement contribution, life and health insurance payments, and educational funds.

Table 11-6: Annual Compensation Of Bookkeeper By Education

Highest Degree	High School	Associate	Bachelor	Master	Doctorate
Number Of Respondents	66	32	46	4	0
Salary (100%*)	25,136	27,023	28,151	26,015	
Annual % Increase (76%)	6%	3%	4%	8%	
Parsonage (0%)	0	0	0	0	
Housing (1%)	14,700	0	0	0	
Retirement (41%)	2,097	2,263	1,663	1,580	
Life Insurance (35%)	453	358	276	496	
Health Insurance (60%)	3,884	4,917	5,069	6,094	
Vacation/weeks (93%)	3	3	3	2	
Education Funds (15%)	448	250	700	1,050	
Auto Allowance (83%)	86%	81%	80%	100%	

* The percentage following each compensation item indicates the portion of all church bookkeepers who received that form of compensation. The averages in each column are for those individuals who actually received that compensation item. See Chapter 3 for a full explanation of how to read this table.

Total Compensation Comparisons

Highest Degree	High School	Associate	Bachelor	Master	Doctorate
Average attendance	1,323	991	1,746	825	
Average church income	1,580,824	1,505,442	2,432,198	1,697,958	
Average years employed	9	9	7	3	
Average compensation*	28,602	30,887	32,378	30,896	
Standard deviation	8,084	9,418	9,529	10,056	
Median compensation	27,400	30,497	32,377	25,000	

National average for all bookkeepers: $30,457 with a standard deviation of $8,769 (see Chapter 4, Table 4-3)

Total respondents: 148

* includes base salary, housing or parsonage allowance, retirement contribution, life and health insurance payments, and educational funds.

Table 11-7: Annual Compensation Of Bookkeeper By Years Employed

Years Employed	0-5	6-10	11-15	over 15
Number Of Respondents	96	44	25	32
Salary (100%*)	26,108	25,759	27,114	29,693
Annual % Increase (76%)	4%	6%	4%	3%
Parsonage (0%)	0	0	0	0
Housing (1%)	0	0	14,700	0
Retirement (41%)	1,800	1,998	2,416	1,751
Life Insurance (35%)	186	631	698	291
Health Insurance (60%)	4,223	5,328	4,018	4,484
Vacation/weeks (93%)	2	3	3	4
Education Funds (15%)	488	733	481	300
Auto Allowance (83%)	84%	80%	80%	88%

* The percentage following each compensation item indicates the portion of all church bookkeepers who received that form of compensation. The averages in each column are for those individuals who actually received that compensation item. See Chapter 3 for a full explanation of how to read this table.

Total Compensation Comparisons

Years Employed	0-5	6-10	11-15	over 15
Average attendance	1,088	1,487	884	1,682
Average church income	1,717,922	1,882,455	1,616,781	2,058,181
Average years employed	3	8	13	21
Average compensation*	29,239	29,646	32,404	33,573
Standard deviation	9,030	9,916	6,970	6,705
Median compensation	28,777	29,000	32,585	32,377

National average for all bookkeepers: $30,457 with a standard deviation of $8,769 (see Chapter 4, Table 4-3)

Total respondents: 197

* includes base salary, housing or parsonage allowance, retirement contribution, life and health insurance payments, and educational funds.

Table 11-8: Annual Compensation Of Part-Time Bookkeepers By Hours Worked

Hours-per-week	1-14	15-29	30-39	All Part-time
Number Of Respondents	27	58	19	214
Salary (100%*)	4,755	13,122	23,257	11,246
Annual % Increase (64%)	4	7	6	5
Parsonage (0%)	0	0	0	0
Housing (0%)	0	0	0	0
Retirement (9%)	1,260	787	2,584	1,895
Life Insurance (4%)	0	100	1,613	1,074
Health Insurance (5%)	1,785	2,996	3,461	3,140
Vacation/weeks (42%)	3	3	2	2
Education Funds (5%)	500	312	0	369
Auto Allowance (75%)	89	91	84	75

* The percentage following each compensation item indicates the portion of all part-time church bookkeepers who received that form of compensation. The averages in each column are for those individuals who actually received that compensation item. See Chapter 3 for a full explanation of how to read this table.

Total Compensation Comparisons

Hours Worked Per Week	1-14	15-29	30-39	All Part-time
Average attendance	406	747	1,129	593
Average church income	521,199	987,957	1,534,111	888,842
Average years employed	6	7	7	6
Average hours per week	8	21	31	19
Average compensation	4,891	13,398	25,591	11,652
Average hourly compensation*	11.76	12.27	15.88	11.79
Average hourly salary	11.43	12.02	14.43	11.38

Total respondents: 214

* includes base salary, housing or parsonage allowance, retirement contribution, life and health insurance payments, and educational funds.

** includes base salary only; see discussion on "rounding errors" in Chapter 3.

Chapter 12

Church Secretaries

Employment Profile

The title of church secretary can encompass a number of clerical and administrative roles within the church office. Church secretaries are the second most common paid position on the church staff following pastors. Almost all are church employees with 99% being female. One percent served as ordained ministers, although almost all viewed their work as both a ministry and a job. Most have worked as business secretaries and over 60% work in the church they attend. The secretaries surveyed provided the following employment profile:

	Full-time	Part-time
☐ Number of Respondents	1,288	1,045
☐ Ordained	1%	0%
☐ Average Years Employed	7	6
☐ Male	1%	2%
☐ Female	99%	98%
☐ Self-employed	0%	1%
☐ Church Employee	100%	99%
☐ High School Diploma	57%	60%
☐ Associate Degree	15%	15%
☐ Bachelor Degree	24%	20%
☐ Master Degree	3%	3%
☐ Doctorate	1%	2%

Compensation Analysis

The analysis below is based upon the tables found later in this chapter. The tables present compensation data according to worship attendance, church income, combinations of size and setting, gender, education, and years employed for church secretaries who serve full-time. The final table provides data for part-time church secretaries based upon the number of hours worked. In this way, the church secretary's compensation can be viewed from a variety of useful perspectives. The total compensation amount found in a separate box at the bottom of each page includes the base salary, housing or parsonage amount, life and health insurance payments, retirement contribution, and educational funds.

Key Points

✎ *Secretarial compensation was affected by church size.* Compensation for church secretaries increased gradually with size. The national average compensation corresponded with a church size of about 400 people. Secretaries serving in smaller congregations were paid substantially less than the national average. *See Table 12-1.*

✎ *Church income had an impact on compensation.* Similar to attendance, total compensation increased with church income. The national average compensation was obtained with church incomes approaching $400,000. The biggest increases occurred once church income passed $1,000,000. *See Table 12-2.*

✎ *Suburban and urban churches provided the best compensation for smaller churches.* These churches achieved the national average compensation with an attendance of under 300 people. Churches in other settings paid considerably less, although the fringe benefits were comparable. *See Table 12-3.*

✎ *Urban and suburban churches provided the best compensation for larger churches with an average attendance over 500.* All larger churches provided a compensation package near or above the national average. *See Table 12-4.*

✎ *Over 99% of these church secretaries were women.* The few men who participated in this study reported an annual compensation about the same as that of the women. Yet, the male secretaries in this study tended to serve congregations with smaller incomes. On average, the male secretaries had worked less than their female counterparts. *See Table 12-5.*

✎ *Educational attainment had little impact on compensation.* The true controlling factors were attendance and church income. Those secretaries with college degrees earned more than those who were high school graduates, although it is not clear that the higher income is attributable to education. *See Table 12-6.*

✎ *Years employed had some impact on compensation.* A secretary who had worked thirteen years earned about the same as one who had worked eight years. Over half of these secretaries had worked on average only three years. About 13% had worked more than fifteen years. *See Table 12-7.*

✎ *Part-time secretaries earn less per hour than do their full-time counterparts.* The typical part-time church secretary works about three days per week. Some part-time secretaries do not receive a salary, but rather receive their compensation as fringe benefits. *See Table 12-8.*

Benefit Analysis

Full-time staff members. Church secretaries received less benefits for full-time work than ministerial and professional staff. Housing allowances were negligible. Only 34% received health insurance, less than any other position surveyed in this study.

Part-time staff members. Thirty-nine percent of church secretaries worked part-time. Most work less than 30 hours per week. Ninety-nine percent of church secretaries working part-time were employees of the church and 1% were self-employed. Few benefits were provided for part-time church secretaries apart from paid vacation.

Benefits	Full-time	Part-time
❐ Housing allowance	0%	0%
❐ Parsonage provided	0%	0%
❐ Retirement	23%	5%
❐ Life insurance	11%	1%
❐ Health insurance	33%	5%
❐ Paid vacation	87%	59%
❐ Auto allowance	29%	17%
❐ Continuing education funds	17%	8%

Eleven Year Compensation Trend: National Averages for Church Secretaries

❐	1993	$17,442
❐	1994	$18,595
❐	1995	$18,858
❐	1996	$19,178
❐	1997	$20,232
❐	1998	$20,353
❐	1999	$21,354
❐	2000	$21,965
❐	2001	$23,316
❐	2002	$24,132
❐	2003	$24,875

Table 12-1: Annual Compensation Of Secretary By Worship Attendance

Church Attendance	0-99	100-299	300-499	500-749	750-999	over 1,000
Number Of Respondents	39	499	293	192	89	140
Salary (95%*)	17,982	21,613	22,957	24,438	24,852	26,736
Annual % Increase (64%)	4%	4%	4%	5%	4%	4%
Parsonage (0%)	0	0	0	0	0	0
Housing (0%)	0	0	0	0	0	0
Retirement (23%)	1,505	1,802	1,530	1,708	2,175	1,867
Life Insurance (11%)	123	503	385	303	295	241
Health Insurance (33%)	4,883	3,920	4,070	4,328	4,664	4,813
Vacation/weeks (87%)	2	3	3	3	3	3
Education Funds (17%)	233	362	394	425	346	406
Auto Allowance (29%)	3%	15%	27%	41%	60%	50%

* The percentage following each compensation item indicates the portion of church secretaries who received that form of compensation. The averages in each column are for those individuals who actually received that compensation item. See Chapter 3 for a full explanation of how to read this table.

Total Compensation Comparisons

Church Attendance	0-99	100-299	300-499	500-749	750-999	over 1,000
Average attendance	69	194	368	593	848	2,279
Average church income	143,126	306,314	585,773	1,028,369	1,527,964	2,774,641
Average years employed	8	7	7	7	7	8
Average compensation*	19,537	22,755	24,733	26,424	27,861	30,264
Standard deviation	9,069	12,027	7,704	8,184	7,879	11,743
Median compensation	17,981	21,000	23,965	26,000	26,477	28,413

National average: $24,875 with a standard deviation of $10,440 (see Chapter 4, Table 4-3).

Total respondents: 1,252

* includes base salary, housing or parsonage allowance, retirement contribution, life and health insurance payments, and educational funds.

Table 12-2: Annual Compensation Of Secretary By Church Income

Church Income in $	0-249,999	250,000-499,999	500,000-749,000	750,000-999,999	1,000,000 +
Number Of Respondents	179	333	156	85	262
Salary (95*)	19,010	22,583	24,204	24,563	26,165
Annual % Increase (64%)	4%	4%	4%	4%	4%
Parsonage (0%)	0	0	0	0	0
Housing (0%)	0	0	0	0	0
Retirement (23%)	1,437	1,775	1,673	2,036	1,985
Life Insurance (11%)	539	497	367	199	296
Health Insurance (33%)	3,640	4,135	4,244	4,692	4,589
Vacation/weeks (87%)	3	3	3	3	3
Education Funds (17%)	307	349	525	338	418
Auto Allowance (29%)	12%	18%	34%	55%	64%

* The percentage following each compensation item indicates the portion of church secretaries who received that form of compensation. The averages in each column are for those individuals who actually received that compensation item. See Chapter 3 for a full explanation of how to read this table.

Total Compensation Comparisons

Church Budget	0-249,999	250,000-499,999	500,000-749,999	750,000-999,999	1,000,000+
Average attendance	210	258	454	573	1,379
Average church income	161,800	340,703	587,943	860,770	2,089,889
Average years employed	8	8	7	7	8
Average compensation*	20,155	24,052	26,242	26,917	29,633
Standard deviation	7,205	12,953	6,594	7,201	8,686
Median compensation	19,845	22,415	25,315	26,105	28,809

National average: $24,875 with a standard deviation of $10,440 (see Chapter 4, Table 4-3).

Total respondents: 1,015

* includes base salary, housing or parsonage allowance, retirement contribution, life and health insurance payments, and educational funds.

Table 12-3: Annual Compensation Of Secretary By Church Setting And Size

Attendance Under 500	Urban	Suburban	Medium City	Small Town	Rural
Number Of Respondents	90	219	202	257	43
Salary (95%*)	22,968	24,118	21,488	20,349	20,082
Annual % Increase (64%)	5%	4%	4%	4%	4%
Parsonage (0%)	0	0	0	0	0
Housing (0%)	0	0	0	0	0
Retirement (23%)	2,165	1,592	1,722	1,550	1,254
Life Insurance (11%)	577	446	572	261	119
Health Insurance (33%)	4,616	3,785	4,241	3,788	4,364
Vacation/weeks (87%)	2	3	3	3	3
Education Funds (17%)	453	390	344	364	171
Auto Allowance (29%)	23%	27%	17%	13%	12%

* The percentage following each compensation item indicates the portion of church secretaries who received that form of compensation. The averages in each column are for those individuals who actually received that compensation item. See Chapter 3 for a full explanation of how to read this table.

Total Compensation Comparisons

Attendance Under 500	Urban	Suburban	Medium City	Small Town	Rural
Average attendance	248	264	242	247	225
Average church income	491,894	443,862	377,680	369,285	284,664
Average years employed	6	8	7	8	8
Average compensation*	24,522	25,841	22,646	21,624	20,904
Standard deviation	8,865	9,165	7,903	13,962	7,551
Median compensation	24,000	24,900	21,828	20,748	20,800

National average: $24,875 with a standard deviation of $10,440 (see Chapter 4, Table 4-3).

Total respondents: 811

* includes base salary, housing or parsonage allowance, retirement contribution, life and health insurance payments, and educational funds.

Table 12-4: Annual Compensation Of Secretary By Church Setting And Size

Attendance Over 499	Urban	Suburban	Medium City	Small Town	Rural
Number Of Respondents	62	163	119	53	11
Salary (95%*)	27,622	26,348	24,055	22,794	22,340
Annual % Increase (64%)	4%	4%	5%	5%	3%
Parsonage (0%)	0	0	0	0	0
Housing (0%)	0	0	0	0	0
Retirement (23%)	2,201	2,002	1,559	1,633	2,100
Life Insurance (11%)	225	293	253	322	94
Health Insurance (33%)	3,902	4,655	4,772	5,034	4,558
Vacation/weeks (87%)	3	3	3	2	3
Education Funds (17%)	539	362	286	556	350
Auto Allowance (29%)	47%	55%	45%	43%	55%

* The percentage following each compensation item indicates the portion of church secretaries who received that form of compensation. The averages in each column are for those individuals who actually received that compensation item. See Chapter 3 for a full explanation of how to read this table.

Total Compensation Comparisons

Attendance Over 499	Urban	Suburban	Medium City	Small Town	Rural
Average attendance	1,607	1,317	1,078	756	767
Average church income	2,341,043	1,934,882	1,397,134	1,123,457	1,106,026
Average years employed	6	8	7	7	6
Average compensation*	30,643	29,232	26,903	24,453	25,066
Standard deviation	10,885	9,672	8,663	7,036	7,355
Median compensation	29,000	28,000	26,284	24,265	24,548

National average: $24,875 with a standard deviation of $10,440 (see Chapter 4, Table 4-3).

Total respondents: 408

* includes base salary, housing or parsonage allowance, retirement contribution, life and health insurance payments, and educational funds.

Table 12-5: Annual Compensation Of Secretary By Gender

Gender	Male	Female
Number Of Respondents	14	1,269
Salary (95%*)	23,978	23,000
Annual % Increase (64%)	9%	4%
Parsonage (0%)	0	0
Housing (0%)	0	0
Retirement (23%)	1,087	1,771
Life Insurance (11%)	156	324
Health Insurance (33%)	2,521	4,330
Vacation/weeks (87%)	2	3
Education Funds (17%)	533	377
Auto Allowance (29%)	57%	29%

* The percentage following each compensation item indicates the portion of church secretaries who received that form of compensation. The averages in each column are for those individuals who actually received that compensation item. See Chapter 3 for a full explanation of how to read this table.

Total Compensation Comparisons

Gender	Male	Female
Average attendance	395	574
Average church income	666,525	844,761
Average years employed	3	7
Average compensation*	25,170	24,855
Standard deviation	6,569	10,438
Median compensation	23,725	23,885

National average: $24,875 with a standard deviation of $10,440 (see Chapter 4, Table 4-3).

Total respondents: 1,283

* includes base salary, housing or parsonage allowance, retirement contribution, life and health insurance payments, and educational funds.

Table 12-6: Annual Compensation Of Secretary By Education

Highest Degree	High School	Associate	Bachelor	Master	Doctorate
Number Of Respondents	611	157	268	35	8
Salary (95%*)	22,292	23,350	23,891	24,272	24,063
Annual % Increase (64%)	4%	5%	5%	3%	2%
Parsonage (0%)	0	0	0	0	0
Housing (0%)	0	0	0	0	0
Retirement (23%)	1,741	1,460	1,780	1,595	0
Life Insurance (11%)	285	400	332	61	0
Health Insurance (33%)	4,185	4,430	4,717	3,845	3,744
Vacation/weeks (87%)	3	3	3	2	2
Education Funds (17%)	378	408	391	256	0
Auto Allowance (29%)	24%	18%	27%	26%	0

* The percentage following each compensation item indicates the portion of church secretaries who received that form of compensation. The averages in each column are for those individuals who actually received that compensation item. See Chapter 3 for a full explanation of how to read this table.

Total Compensation Comparisons

Highest Degree	High School	Associate	Bachelor	Master	Doctorate
Average attendance	613	420	546	401	359
Average church income	799,810	567,996	916,025	501,913	609,500
Average years employed	8	7	6	7	5
Average compensation	23,962	24,885	25,801	26,427	24,599
Standard deviation	8,712	17,988	9,316	6,705	10,362
Median compensation	23,000	22,749	25,000	25,000	22,000

National average: $24,875 with a standard deviation of $10,440 (see Chapter 4, Table 4-3).

Total respondents: 1,079

* includes base salary, housing or parsonage allowance, retirement contribution, life and health insurance payments, and educational funds.

Table 12-7: Annual Compensation Of Secretary By Years Employed

Years Employed	0-5	6-10	11-15	over 15
Number Of Respondents	699	261	144	168
Salary (95%*)	22,159	23,338	23,524	25,555
Annual % Increase (64%)	5%	4%	4%	3%
Parsonage (0%)	0	0	0	0
Housing (0%)	0	0	0	0
Retirement (23%)	1,633	1,726	2,007	1,896
Life Insurance (11%)	227	315	513	363
Health Insurance (33%)	4,072	4,112	4,782	4,857
Vacation/weeks (87%)	2	3	3	4
Education Funds (17%)	401	392	350	324
Auto Allowance (29%)	28%	27%	26%	33%

* The percentage following each compensation item indicates the portion of church secretaries who received that form of compensation. The averages in each column are for those individuals who actually received that compensation item. See Chapter 3 for a full explanation of how to read this table.

Total Compensation Comparisons

Years Employed	0-5	6-10	11-15	over 15
Average attendance	512	707	566	566
Average church income	811,113	876,091	740,613	995,537
Average years employed	3	8	13	21
Average compensation*	23,596	25,659	25,702	28,037
Standard deviation	8,622	8,730	8,807	17,618
Median compensation	22,280	24,500	25,000	26,450

National average: $24,875 with a standard deviation of $10,440 (see Chapter 4, Table 4-3).

Total respondents: 1,272

* includes base salary, housing or parsonage allowance, retirement contribution, life and health insurance payments, and educational funds.

Table 12-8: Annual Compensation Of Part-Time Secretaries By Hours Worked

Hours-per-week	under 15	15-29	30-39	All Part-time
Number Of Respondents	72	590	221	1,045**
Salary (94%*)	5,934	10,922	17,212	12,049
Annual % Increase (51%)	5%	5%	5%	5%
Parsonage (0%)	0	0	0	0
Housing (0%)	0	0	0	0
Retirement (5%)	0	1,334	1,610	1,537
Life Insurance (1%)	0	414	298	333
Health Insurance (5%)	4,300	2,711	4,307	3,564
Vacation/weeks (59%)	2	2	2	2
Education Funds (8%)	0	237	233	245
Auto Allowance (17%)	14%	12%	14%	17%

* The percentage following each compensation item indicates the portion of part-time church secretaries who received that form of compensation. The averages in each column are for those individuals who actually received that compensation item. See Chapter 3 for a full explanation of how to read this table.

Total Compensation Comparisons

Hours Worked Per Week	under 15	15-29	30-39	All Part-time
Average attendance	117	247	291	249
Average church income	159,429	279,666	353,087	304,910
Average years employed	5	5	6	6
Average hours per week	10	21	31	23
Average compensation	6,004	11,040	17,833	12,320
Ave. hourly compensation*	11.55	10.11	11.06	10.30
Average hourly salary**	11.41	10.00	10.68	10.07

Total respondents: 1,045

* includes base salary, housing or parsonage allowance, retirement contribution, life and health insurance payments, and educational funds.

** includes base salary; see discussion on "rounding errors" in Chapter 3.

Chapter 13

Church Custodians

Employment profile

Church custodians normally receive an hourly wage and function as church employees. Most are men, although women represent 46% of those working part-time. Some custodians are ordained ministers. The custodians surveyed provided the following employment profile:

Respondents:	Full-time	Part-time
☐ Number of Respondents	298	301
☐ Ordained	1%	0%
☐ Average Years Employed	7	6
☐ Male	84%	54%
☐ Female	16%	46%
☐ Self-employed	0%	10%
☐ Church Employee	100%	90%
☐ High School Diploma	83%	85%
☐ Associate's Degree	4%	1%
☐ Bachelor's Degree	10%	12%
☐ Master's Degree	3%	2%
☐ Doctorate	0%	0%

Compensation Analysis

The analysis below is based upon the tables found later in this chapter. The tables present compensation data according to worship attendance, church income, combinations of size and setting, gender, education, and years employed for church custodians who serve full-time. The final table provides data for part-time church custodians based upon the number of hours worked. In this way, the church custodian's compensation can be viewed from a variety of useful perspectives. The total compensation amount found in a separate box at the bottom of each page includes the base salary, housing or parsonage amount, life and health insurance payments, retirement contribution, and educational funds.

Key Points

✎ *Compensation increased gradually with church size.* The national average compensation corresponded to a church size of about 700 people. *See Table 13-1.*

✎ *The church's income was more of a predictor of compensation than was church size.* Compensation increased steadily with church income. The highest compensation levels occurred when churches had incomes over $1,000,000. *See Table 13-2.*

✎ *Urban and suburban churches provided the best income for churches with an average attendance below 500.* Yet in this group, all churches were below the national average. *See Table 13-3.*

✎ *More parity existed among churches with an average attendance above 500.* All congregations with an attendance above 500 provided compensation levels above the national average, except for those in rural settings. *See Table 13-4.*

✎ *A significant difference existed in compensation levels between men and women.* On average, females earned 67% of their male counterparts. In general, men earned about $10,000 per year more than did women. Males worked in larger congregations, with more income than the congregations in which the female custodians served, but the differences are not enough to account for the disparity in compensation. *See Table 13-5.*

✎ *Most custodians are high school graduates.* About 12% were college graduates. In general, compensation increases for those with higher education. This is not always the case, however, and in some years, such as this one, those with a master's degree earn less than those with a high school education. *See Table 13-6.*

✎ *Compensation increased somewhat with years served.* Those serving on average thirteen years earned about $1,800 more than those who had worked on average eight years. Those with five or less years of service earned below the national average. *See Table 13-7.*

✎ *On an hourly basis, part-time custodians earn less per hour than their full-time counterparts.* Most part-time custodians work about 17 hours per week. *See Table 13-8.*

Benefit Analysis

Full-time staff members. Church custodians received fewer and smaller benefits than full-time ministerial or professional staff. Over half received health insurance, but only 40% had any retirement program from the church. Benefits received were about the same as bookkeepers and more than secretaries.

Part-time church staff. About the same number of church custodians worked part-time as full-time. Forty-eight percent were part-time employees. Of this group, 46% were women. Ten percent of the part-time custodians were self-employed. Churches provided part-time custodial workers very few benefits as compared to full-time employees. Part-time custodial work is primarily a straight hourly wage position.

Benefits	Full-time	Part-time
☐ Housing allowance	0%	0%
☐ Parsonage provided	1%	0%
☐ Retirement	40%	1%
☐ Life insurance	32%	1%
☐ Health insurance	62%	2%
☐ Paid vacation	91%	32%
☐ Auto allowance	85%	57%
☐ Continuing educational funds	6%	1%

Eleven Year Compensation Trend: National Averages for Church Custodians

☐	1993	$18,617
☐	1994	$20,541
☐	1995	$20,161
☐	1996	$21,608
☐	1997	$22,493
☐	1998	$23,271
☐	1999	$24,401
☐	2000	$26,161
☐	2001	$26,725
☐	2002	$27,913
☐	2003	$29,047

Table 13-1: Annual Compensation Of Custodian By Worship Attendance

Church Attendance	0-99	100-299	300-499	500-749	750-999	over 1,000
Number	4	41	56	56	43	90
Salary (100%*)	10,456	19,408	23,104	24,768	26,716	28,722
Annual % Increase (75%)	3%	5%	3%	4%	3%	4%
Parsonage (1%)	0	0	0	0	0	6,000
Housing (0%)	0	0	0	0	0	0
Retirement (40%)	0	1,750	2,020	1,607	1,758	1,803
Life Insurance (32%)	0	326	709	203	1,248	192
Health Insurance (62%)	0	3,521	4,783	4,635	6,608	4,988
Vacation/weeks (91%)	2	2	3	3	3	3
Education Funds (6%)	0	200	500	312	600	347
Auto Allowance (85%)	50%	63%	91%	89%	86%	88%

* The percentage following each compensation item indicate the portion of church custodians who received that form of compensation. The averages in each column are for those individuals who actually received that compensation item. See Chapter 3 for a full explanation of how to read this table.

Total Compensation Comparisons At A Glance

Worship Attendance	0-99	100-299	300-499	500-749	750-999	over 1,000
Average attendance	74	211	390	589	847	2,323
Average church income	104,667	431,229	826,222	1,180,246	1,777,831	2,987,993
Average years employed	6	6	7	7	8	7
Average compensation*	10,456	21,527	26,781	28,319	31,845	33,737
Standard deviation	5,599	8,775	9,206	9,435	8,164	9,628
Median compensation	7,900	20,899	25,446	28,300	31,944	30,650

National average for all custodians: $29,047 with a standard deviation of $10,260 (see Chapter 4, Table 4-3)

Total respondents: 290

* includes base salary, housing or parsonage allowance, retirement contributions, life and health insurance payments, and educational funds.

Table 13-2: Annual Compensation Of Custodian By Church Budget

Church Budget in $	0-249,999	250,000-499,999	500,000-749,000	750,000-999,999	1,000,000 +
Number Of Respondents	14	30	34	33	165
Salary (100%*)	14,736	18,950	22,155	25,918	27,469
Annual % Increase (75%)	3%	4%	4%	3%	4%
Parsonage (1%)	0	0	0	0	8,200
Housing (0%)	0	0	0	0	0
Retirement (40%)	1,590	1,045	1,470	2,160	1,916
Life Insurance (32%)	130	371	451	226	496
Health Insurance (62%)	3,308	3,275	4,818	5,655	5,171
Vacation/weeks (91%)	2	2	2	3	3
Education Funds (6%)	0	350	0	200	448
Auto Allowance (85%)	64%	67%	85%	91%	88%

* The percentage following each compensation item indicate the portion of church custodians who received that form of compensation. The averages in each column are for those individuals who actually received that compensation item. See Chapter 3 for a full explanation of how to read this table.

Total Compensation Comparisons

Church Budget	0-249,000	250,000-499,999	500,000-749,999	750,000-999,999	1,000,000+
Average attendance	293	269	373	619	1,531
Average church income	152,011	393,324	637,408	845,816	2,326,270
Average years employed	10	5	6	8	8
Average compensation*	15,331	20,807	24,964	30,634	32,335
Standard deviation	9,521	6,818	7,724	11,607	9,174
Median compensation	13,000	20,899	26,705	29,200	30,400

National average for all custodians: $29,047 with a standard deviation of $10,260 (see Chapter 4, Table 4-3)

Total respondents: 276

* includes base salary, housing or parsonage allowance, retirement contributions, life and health insurance payments, and educational funds.

Table 13-3: Annual Compensation Of Custodian By Church Setting And Size

Attendance Under 500	Urban	Suburban	Medium City	Small Town	Rural
Number Of Respondents	13	32	24	26	3
Salary (100%*)	21,586	25,034	19,319	17,323	21,927
Annual % Increase (75%)	4%	4%	4%	4%	6%
Parsonage (1%)	0	0	0	0	0
Housing (0%)	0	0	0	0	0
Retirement (40%)	2,469	2,029	1,272	1,711	0
Life Insurance (32%)	1,456	433	480	72	0
Health Insurance (62%)	3,835	4,904	4,374	4,220	0
Vacation/weeks (91%)	3	2	2	2	2
Education Funds (6%)	500	200	0	0	0
Auto Allowance (85%)	100%	81%	83%	62%	67%

* The percentage following each compensation item indicate the portion of church custodians who received that form of compensation. The averages in each column are for those individuals who actually received that compensation item. See Chapter 3 for a full explanation of how to read this table.

Total Compensation Comparisons

Attendance Under 500	Urban	Suburban	Medium City	Small Town	Rural
Average attendance	313	325	291	279	376
Average church income	892,523	702,267	592,863	534,429	458,800
Average years employed	7	6	6	9	3
Average compensation*	26,562	28,451	21,592	19,019	21,997
Standard deviation	6,825	12,036	6,217	7,650	5,866
Median compensation	26,528	27,980	20,867	19,900	16,212

National average for all custodians: $29,047 with a standard deviation of $10,260 (see Chapter 4, Table 4-3)

Total respondents: 98

* includes base salary, housing or parsonage allowance, retirement contributions, life and health insurance payments, and educational funds.

Table 13-4: Annual Compensation Of Custodian By Church Setting And Size

Attendance Over 499	Urban	Suburban	Medium City	Small Town	Rural
Number Of Respondents	27	81	54	18	7
Salary (100%*)	27,818	27,886	26,188	26,633	23,316
Annual % Increase (75%)	5%	4%	4%	4%	4%
Parsonage (1%)	0	10,400	6,000	0	0
Housing (0%)	0	0	0	0	0
Retirement (40%)	1,786	1,875	1,457	1,810	0
Life Insurance (32%)	233	383	624	153	98
Health Insurance (62%)	4,888	5,270	5,150	4,712	6,619
Vacation/weeks (91%)	3	3	3	2	2
Education Funds (6%)	638	405	288	233	0
Auto Allowance (85%)	85%	89%	85%	89%	100%

* The percentage following each compensation item indicate the portion of church custodians who received that form of compensation. The averages in each column are for those individuals who actually received that compensation item. See Chapter 3 for a full explanation of how to read this table.

Total Compensation Comparisons

Attendance Over 499	Urban	Suburban	Medium City	Small Town	Rural
Average attendance	1,868	1,636	1,339	926	801
Average church income	3,136,463	2,374,090	1,585,779	1,829,981	1,134,571
Average years employed	8	7	7	6	5
Average compensation*	32,637	32,502	30,605	31,341	27,126
Standard deviation	8,173	10,230	9,222	8,141	12,211
Median compensation	31,844	30,298	28,316	29,683	27,450

National average for all custodians: $29,047 with a standard deviation of $10,260 (see Chapter 4, Table 4-3)

Total respondents: 187

* includes base salary, housing or parsonage allowance, retirement contributions, life and health insurance payments, and educational funds.

Table 13-5: Annual Compensation Of Custodian By Gender

Gender	Male	Female
Number Of Respondents	250	48
Salary (100%*)	26,345	18,394
Annual % Increase (75%)	4%	4%
Parsonage (1%)	8,200	0
Housing (0%)	0	0
Retirement (40%)	1,812	1,561
Life Insurance (32%)	449	200
Health Insurance (62%)	4,954	4,629
Vacation/weeks (91%)	3	2
Education Funds (6%)	396	0
Auto Allowance (85%)	87%	73%

* The percentage following each compensation item indicate the portion of church custodians who received that form of compensation. The averages in each column are for those individuals who actually received that compensation item. See Chapter 3 for a full explanation of how to read this table.

Total Compensation Comparisons

Gender	Male	Female
Average attendance	1,125	763
Average church income	1,641,932	1,509,501
Average years employed	7	8
Average compensation*	30,652	20,684
Standard deviation	9,860	8,060
Median compensation	29,683	21,000

National average for all custodians: $29,047 with a standard deviation of $10,260 (see Chapter 4, Table 4-3)

Total respondents: 298

* includes base salary, housing or parsonage allowance, retirement contributions, life and health insurance payments, and educational funds.

Table 13-6: Annual Compensation Of Custodian By Education

Highest Degree	High School	Associate	Bachelor	Master	Doctorate
Number Of Respondents	149	8	17	5	0
Salary (100%*)	24,805	27,296	27,708	24,895	
Annual % Increase (75%)	4%	4%	4%	3%	
Parsonage (1%)	0	0	0	0	
Housing (0%)	0	0	0	0	
Retirement (40%)	1,732	3,060	1,965	1,954	
Life Insurance (32%)	436	324	200	0	
Health Insurance (62%)	4,544	2,377	5,661	3,851	
Vacation/weeks (91%)	3	3	3	3	
Education Funds (6%)	473	300	0	0	
Auto Allowance (85%)	88%	75%	76%	60%	

* The percentage following each compensation item indicate the portion of church custodians who received that form of compensation. The averages in each column are for those individuals who actually received that compensation item. See Chapter 3 for a full explanation of how to read this table.

Total Compensation Comparisons

Highest Degree	High School	Associate	Bachelor	Master	Doctorate
Average attendance	1,350	1,305	614	367	
Average church income	1,891,865	1,710,614	1,358,080	714,862	
Average years employed	7	4	7	4	
Average compensation*	28,737	28,733	31,858	27,217	
Standard deviation	8,747	11,980	9,646	13,226	
Median compensation	27,631	28,000	30,612	20,000	

National average for all custodians: $29,047 with a standard deviation of $10,260 (see Chapter 4, Table 4-3)

Total respondents: 179

* includes base salary, housing or parsonage allowance, retirement contributions, life and health insurance payments, and educational funds.

Table 13-7: Annual Compensation Of Custodian By Years Employed

Years Employed	0-5	6-10	11-15	over 15
Number Of Respondents	151	78	29	32
Salary (100%*)	24,231	25,762	27,462	25,827
Annual % Increase (75%)	4%	4%	3%	3%
Parsonage (1%)	10,400	6,000	0	0
Housing (0%)	0	0	0	0
Retirement (40%)	1,526	1,758	1,691	2,211
Life Insurance (32%)	590	221	326	267
Health Insurance (62%)	4,793	4,702	5,029	5,644
Vacation/weeks (91%)	2	3	3	4
Education Funds (6%)	285	612	450	462
Auto Allowance (85%)	89%	81%	79%	84%

* The percentage following each compensation item indicate the portion of church custodians who received that form of compensation. The averages in each column are for those individuals who actually received that compensation item. See Chapter 3 for a full explanation of how to read this table.

Total Compensation Comparisons

Years Employed	0-5	6-10	11-15	over 15
Average attendance	1,088	978	1,484	959
Average church income	1,460,534	1,945,556	1,655,149	1,703,899
Average years employed	3	8	13	22
Average compensation*	27,763	29,836	31,691	31,356
Standard deviation	9,626	10,127	9,383	12,554
Median compensation	27,319	28,032	30,285	32,063

National average for all custodians: $29,047 with a standard deviation of $10,260 (see Chapter 4, Table 4-3)

Total respondents: 290

* includes base salary, housing or parsonage allowance, retirement contributions, life and health insurance payments, and educational funds.

Table 13-8: Annual Compensation Of Part-Time Custodians By Hours Worked

Hours-per-week	1-14	15-29	30-39	All Part-time
Number Of Respondents	43	51	16	301
Salary (100%*)	5,155	10,031	16,028	8,711
Annual % Increase (53%)	5%	6%	5%	5%
Parsonage (0%)	0	0	0	0
Housing (0%)	0	0	0	0
Retirement (1%)	0	1,184	0	1,380
Life Insurance (1%)	0	0	0	202
Health Insurance (2%)	994	0	2,234	3,421
Vacation/weeks (32%)	2	2	2	2
Education Funds (1%)	0	0	131	240
Auto Allowance (57%)	74%	84%	94%	57%

* The percentage following each compensation item indicate the portion of part-time church custodians who received that form of compensation. The averages in each column are for those individuals who actually received that compensation item. See Chapter 3 for a full explanation of how to read this table.

Total Compensation Comparisons

Hours Worked Per Week	1-14	15-29	30-39	All Part-time
Average attendance	237	342	493	254
Average church income	270,669	638,699	543,399	388,013
Average years employed	5	5	5	6
Average hours per week	8	20	31	17
Average compensation	5,201	10,054	16,324	8,809
Ave. hourly compensation*	12.50	9.67	10.13	9.96
Average hourly salary**	12.39	9.65	9.94	9.85

Total respondents: 301

* includes base salary, housing or parsonage allowance, retirement contributions, life and health insurance payments, and educational funds.

Includes base salary only; see discussion on "rounding errors" in Chapter 3.

Chapter 14

Statistical Abstract of Participating Churches

In addition to the individual compensation surveys, many of the participating churches also completed a congregational profile. That information is presented below. Data is presented according to Sunday worship attendance. Five size categories are portrayed. Second, attendance and income trends are presented according to both church *size* and *setting*.

Key Findings

☐ Congregations with a Sunday morning worship attendance between 501-750 experienced the highest per capita giving.

☐ On average, 47% of the church budget is devoted to salaries.

☐ About 38% of churches provide additional salary to their ordained staff members to assist them with their social security payments. Of those churches that do help, 37% pay one-half of the social security tax while 49% pay all of it.

☐ Eighty-nine percent of the participating churches reimburse the professional expenses of their ordained employees. The average reimbursement was $3,257, down from $3,534 last year, and $3,774 two years ago.

☐ The majority of churches (94%) require a full accounting of professional expenses including date, purpose, location, and amount of expense before a reimbursement is made.

☐ A high percentage (94%) of churches in our sample were connected to the Internet. This was the same as last year, but up up from 91% two yeas ago and 83% three years ago. The likelihood of being connected increases with church size.

☐ For the first time since 1993, a majority of congregations did not experience an increase in church attendance over the past three years. However, a majority of congregations with an attendance over 500 reported continued growth.

☐ Forty-two percent of the participating churches reported that their income exceeded expenses during the past year. That percentage has now decreased for three consecutive years following seven straight years of growth. Three years ago it was 58%, two years ago it was 55%, and last year it was 47%.

Congregational Profile By Church Worship Attendance

	All n=886	0-250 n=374	251-500 n=213	501-750 n=116	751-1000 n=66	over 1000 n=107
Worship Attendance	571	149	375	628	886	2,421
Total income	$882,933	$247,985	$693,079	$1,198,389	$1,657,045	$2,946,715
Per capita: attendance	$1,546	$1,664	$1,848	$1,908	$1,870	$1,217
What percentage are salaries of your total church budget?	47%	48%	46%	47%	49%	47%
Number of Ordained Staff Full-time/Part-time	3/1	1/1	3/1	3/1	5/2	6/2
Number of Nonordained Staff Full-time/Part-time	6/6	2/3	3/5	6/8	9/10	15/17
Contributes to social security payments of ordained staff	38%	38%	43%	33%	29%	37%
Pays all	49%	45%	46%	54%	65%	55%
Pays half	37%	36%	46%	32%	29%	24%
Reimburses professional expenses (average amount reimbursed)	89% $3,257	85% $2,729	90% $3,413	89% $3,847	91% $4,046	91% $3,454
Requires a full accounting including date, purpose, location and amount before reimbursing expenses	94%	91%	96%	94%	100%	99%
Church has a connection to the Internet	94%	87%	99%	98%	98%	100%
Individual completing questionnaire has a connection to the Internet at home	91%	87%	91%	97%	97%	99%

Attendance and Income Trends by Church Size

Attendance Trend Over the Past Three Years	Decline	Stable	Increase
All Churches (886)	15%	39%	46%
0-250 (374)	21%	43%	36%
251-500 (213)	12%	41%	47%
501-750 (116)	14%	35%	51%
751-1000 (66)	11%	36%	53%
over 1000 (93)	8%	26%	66%

Financial Status	Income below expenses	Income meets expenses	Income above expenses
All churches (886)	23%	35%	42%
0-250 (374	28%	38%	34%
251-500 (213)	21%	34%	45%
501-750 (116)	21%	30%	49%
751-1000 (66)	18%	32%	50%
over 1000 (93)	12%	33%	55%

Attendance and Income Trends by Geographical Setting

Attendance Trend Over the Past Three Years	Decline	Stable	Increase
All Churches (886)	15%	39%	46%
Urban (108)	21%	43%	36%
Suburban (320)	16%	32%	52%
Medium Size City (195)	13%	42%	45%
Small Town (201)	13%	42%	45%
Rural (53)	19%	46%	35%

Financial Status	Income below expenses	Income meets expenses	Income above expenses
All Churches (886)	23%	35%	42%
Urban (108)	30%	30%	40%
Suburban (320)	24%	34%	41%
Medium Size City (195)	22%	37%	41%
Small Town (201)	20%	39%	41%
Rural (53)	19%	28%	53%

Appendix 1

Nine Year Compensation Trend

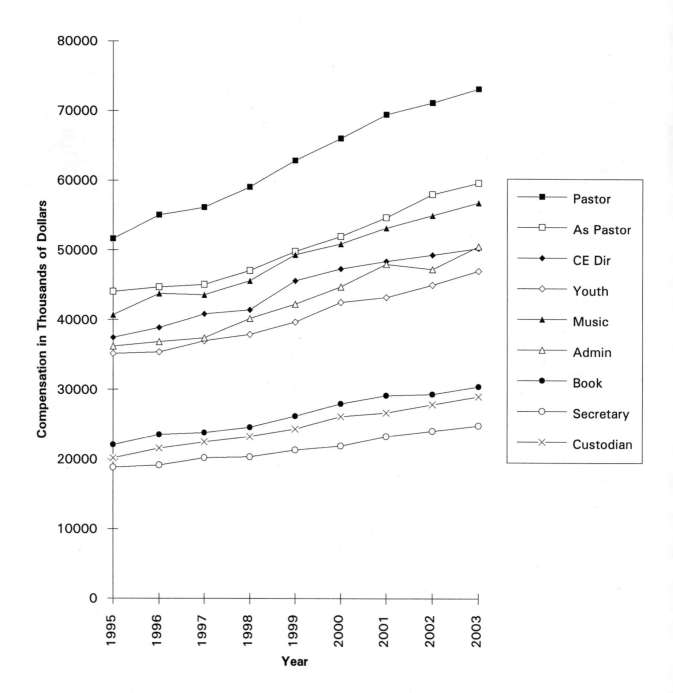

Appendix 2

Standard Deviation Ranges for Pastoral Compensation Based on Church Income

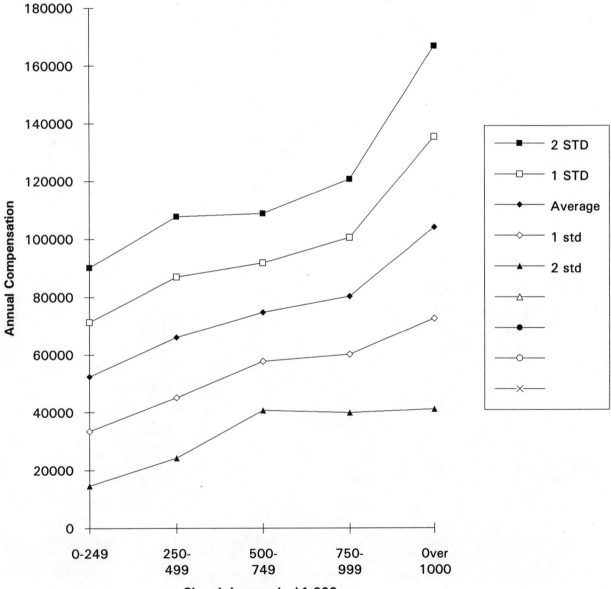

Appendix 3

Compensation and Church Attendance

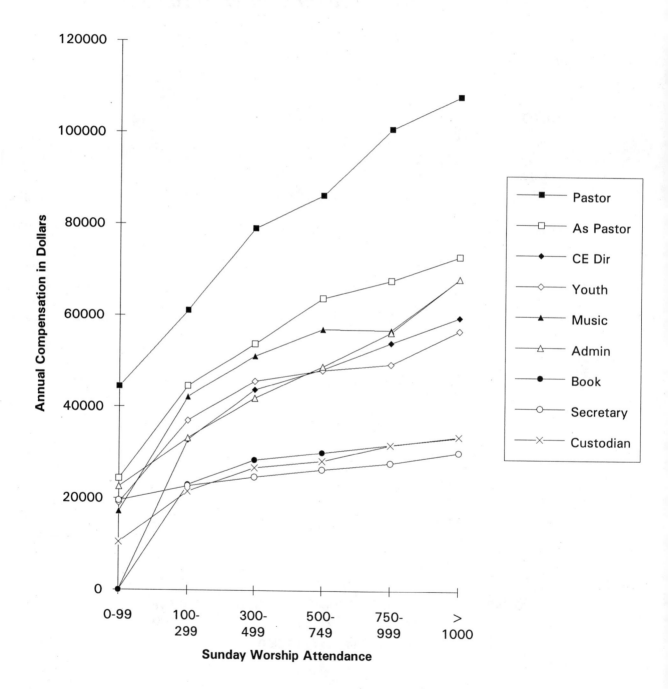

Appendix 4

Compensation Averages by Education

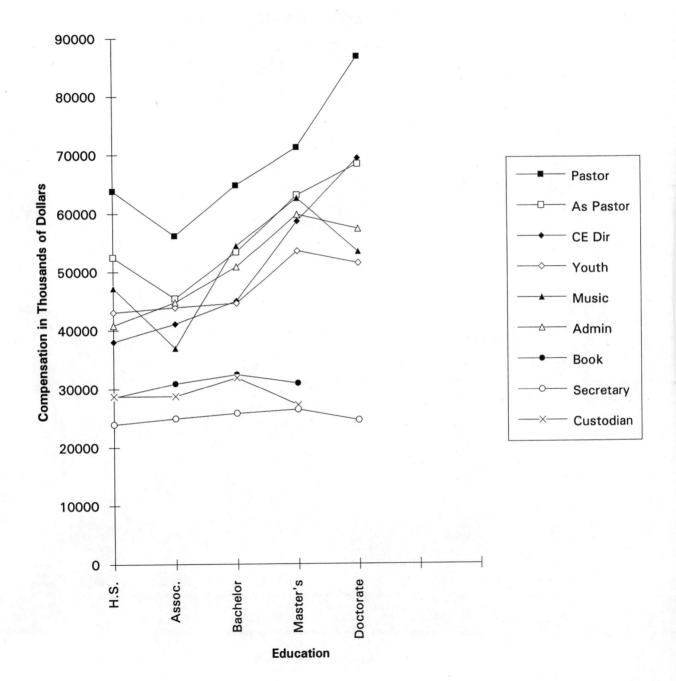

Appendix 5

Standard Deviation Ranges for Pastoral Compensation Based on Church Income

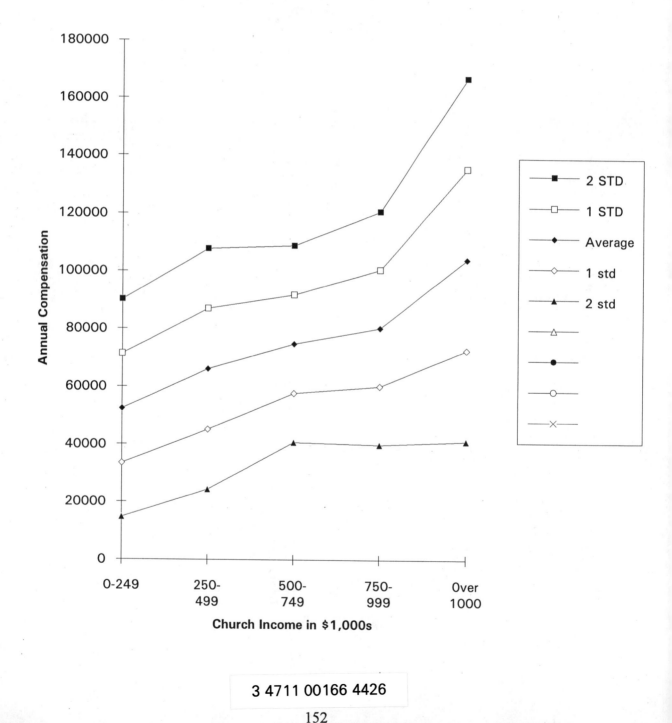